UNIVERSAL STITCHES

for
weaving, embroidery, and other fiber arts

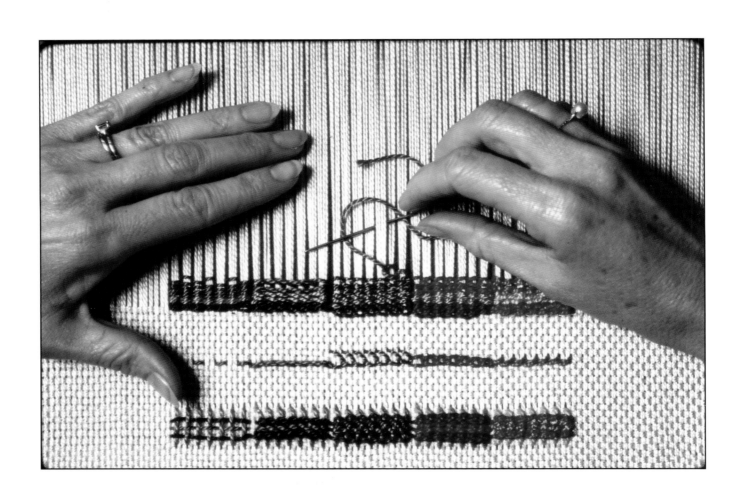

UNIVERSAL STITCHES

for
weaving, embroidery, and other fiber arts

by

NANCY ARTHUR HOSKINS

Schiffer Publishing Ltd

4880 Lower Valley Road • Atglen, PA 19310

DEDICATION To my mother, Ellen Dorothea Lindsay and to my father, Gilbert Veall Arthur

Originally published in 1982 by Skein Publications, Eugene, Oregon
Second printing in 1985 by Skein Publications, Distributed by the University of Washington Press, Seattle and London
Original Design by J. Paul Dusseault, Bryan Sabin, and Rina Boodman of Industrial Litho, Eugene, OR

Library of Congress Control Number: 2012954709

ISBN: 978-0-7643-4431-2

Printed in China

ACKNOWLEDGEMENTS

I wish to express my sincere thanks to . . .

. . . Jack Lenor Larsen for permission to reprint his poem "Time Was and Is" in its original calligraphic form.

The Stanford University Museum of Art and Nancy Bavour,
The Seattle Art Museum and Joice Gail-McKeown,
The Metropolitan Museum of Art and Alice Zriebice,
The University of Washington Textile Study Collection and Krista Turnbull and Virginia Harvey,
The California Academy of Sciences and Joan Bacharach,
The University of Oregon Natural History Museum and Alice Carnes and Betsy Hennings
. . . for allowing me to study the Ancient Egyptian, Coptic, European, Chinese, Peruvian, and American Indian fabrics in their respective collections.

Alda Vinson, art historian, fiber artist, and weaving instructor at Lane Community College,
Dr. Esther Jacobson, Head of the Art History Depatment, Dr. Gordon Kensler, Professor Emeritus of the Art Education Department, and Barbara Pickett, Assistant Professor of Weaving in the Fine Arts Department at the University of Oregon,
Naomi Whiting Towner, Professor of Art, Head of Fiber Program, Illinois State University
. . . all who helped in the initial phase of this work.

. . . Annabel Polk, Jean Cook, Kathrine Weaver, and Lewa Ager for their generous gifts of old needlelace.

. . . those who attended workshops and lectures on this subject at Convergence '78, the Pacific Northwest Handweavers Conference '81, The Handweavers Guilds of Boise, Olympia, Portland, and Eugene, The Eugene Stitchery Guild, and the University of Oregon Summer Session '81.

. . . those who permitted their work to be illustrated in this book—Penelope Drooker, Genie Langdon, Ardis Letey, Helen Richards, Pam Stout, Helen Brent, Alda Vinson, and all of those anonymous artisans from the past.

. . . J. Paul Dusseault, Bryan Sabin, and Rina Boodman of Industrial Litho for their guidance through the process of designing and printing this book.

. . . Oscar Palmquist for help with photography, Julie Koerner for typing assistance, and Judy Harold for reviewing the manuscript.

. . . My brothers and sisters—Audrey, Edwin, Dotty, Jean, and Gilbert for sharing so willingly in family responsibilities.

. . . My husband, Blaine, and to my children, Nanette, Matthew, Karen, and Lisa for their practical advice, wit, wisdom, and loving support throughout this project.

Schiffer Books are available at special discounts for bulk purchases for sales promotions or premiums. Special editions, including personalized covers, corporate imprints, and excerpts can be created in large quantities for special needs. For more information contact the publisher:

Published by Schiffer Publishing, Ltd.
4880 Lower Valley Road
Atglen, PA 19310
Phone: (610) 593-1777; Fax: (610) 593-2002
E-mail: Info@schifferbooks.com

For the largest selection of fine reference books on this and related subjects, please visit our website at
www.schifferbooks.com

CONTENTS

TIME WAS AND IS

TIME WAS AND IS WHEN
A CRAFTSMAN KNEW·
KNEW FABRIC AS FLEECE,
AS CARDED
SLIVER AND YARN,
AS THE MAGIC OF INTERLACINGS,
AND (AFTER SCOURING
AND FINISHING)
AS ONE BARBED
FIBER MESHED WITH MILLIONS
LIKE IT·

FOR A VERY LONG TIME NOW
THESE ASPECTS OF FABRIC
HAVE FOREIGN TO EACH
BEEN OTHER,
SO SEPARATED BY THEIR TYPE AND
CONSTRUCTION, FIBER,
END USE AND MARKET,
THAT WE ARE DEPRIVED
OF THEIR ESSENTIAL CONNECTION·

FOR A MOMENT, LET'S SEE THE
NOT JUST THE WHOLE CLOTH·
'LOOK' OF STUFFS
—THE
SHIMMER, LUSTER, NUB, SLUB, LOOP,
GRAIN AND CORD
OF THEM,
THEIR CREPE & CRINKLE,
PATTERN AND IRIDESCENCE—
BUT THEIR
HANDLE, DRAPE AND RESILIENCE,
THEIR CANDLE AGAINST LIGHT·

ABOVE ALL HONOR THE STRUCTURES:
THOSE ANCIENT LAWS
ALMOST AS BASIC AS FIRE,
MORE UNIVERSAL AND SOMETIMES
EARLIER
THAN THE WHEEL·

SEE FABRIC AS SKIN, AS TRACERY
AND AS DIAPHANOUS
VEILS THICK AND THIN,
SOUND PRIVACY
ABSORBING, LIGHT REFLECTING, MAKING,
AND AS COTTON CLOTHS
SO COMMON AS TO RELATE LAPPS TO LUAUS·

NOW
AND THEN ACKNOWLEDGE
FABRIC WHICH SERVES:
INDUSTRIAL CLOTHS SOMETIMES
VERY BEAUTIFUL
SILKS AND FURS SO SUMPTUOUS
AS TO MAKE AGING MORE
TOLERABLE
FABRICS THAT PERSONALIZE & DIFFERENTIATE
INTERIOR SPACES
AND MAKE INDOOR LIVES
IN CITIES MORE BEARABLE·

NOW WHEN ALL CONNECTIONS
ARE VAGUE
OFTEN SHODDY, MORE OFTEN
ADHESIVE THAN COHESIVE,
IT IS IMPERATIVE THAT DESIGNERS
UNDERSTAND IN THEIR
BONES
THE INTERRELATIONSHIPS
OF THE WHOLE TO THE PARTS·

TO PERCEIVE EVERY PUZZLE PIECE FITS—
THAT
EVEN THE CRASS, SLEAZY ONES,
ASSUME FOR A HIGH VANTAGE POINT·
NOW
WHEN ALL PARTS ARE
IN PLACE, YOU SHALL KNOW·
AND THIS
KNOWLEDGE WILL BECOME AN ASPECT
OF YOUR
INNERMOST EXPERIENCE·

JACK LENOR LARSEN

Introduction

Universal Stitches for Weaving, Embroidery, and Other Fiber Arts teaches how five basic stitches, their variations and combinations, work upon warp and upon fabric in functional and decorative ways with infinite variety. This integrated method of learning is designed to be useful for fiber artists at all levels of experience—beginning to advanced. The heritage of the past is tied to the future of the art fabric with traditional techniques from ancient Egypt, China, and Peru translated for the contemporary craftsman. The text is divided into three main sections: for instruction, inspiration, and information.

"The Learning Projects" outlines the materials and methods for a series of samples and samplers done with loom and non-loom techniques for novice or experienced weavers, and for non-weavers.

"An Album of Ideas" suggests ways of combining the crafts of weaving and embroidery. This section is illustrated with ancient, antique, and contemporary art fabrics to act as a catalyst to creativity.

"The Stitches" begins with an explanation of how the stitches, stitch families, and diagram pages are organized. Then step-by-step directions and diagrams for two hundred stitches—the basic five plus some of their variations and combinations—make up the rest of the book. That section is designed to serve as an index of stitches.

A clarification of terms is necessary for cross-communication between the crafts of weaving and embroidery. A 'stitch' is a structural unit. 'Stitch' refers to that structural unit formed when one element binds to another—the "essential connection"[1]—in the construction of fabric. 'Stitch' also refers to that structural unit formed by an element working upon fabric. A 'constructional stitch' builds fabric. An 'accessory stitch' is added to fabric.[2] There are constructional and accessory versions for each of the five basic stitches and for many others. Both constructional and accessory stitches adhere to the principles of interlacing,[3] wrapping,[4] looping,[5] chaining,[6] and knotting.[7]

The order of the five stitches is a continuum based on structure. The stitch continuum describes the increasing complexity of a stitch as it interlaces, wraps, loops, chains, and knots upon an element, a set of elements, or upon fabric. (fig. 1)

'Stitching' is used to refer not only to sewing, but to the interworking of weft and warp when it is manually controlled with or without a needle or other tool.[8]

'Element' is used as a general term for a yarn or thread.[9] 'Fabric' is a general term for woven textiles and also those constructed with non-weaving methods—felt, baskets, knits, lace, nets, etc.[10]

The structural interrelationship between stitches is used as the basis for a teaching method in this book. It is a nontraditional, but logical way to learn stitches. Because the basic stitches are universal, there is a carry-over to other fiber crafts. An understanding of universal

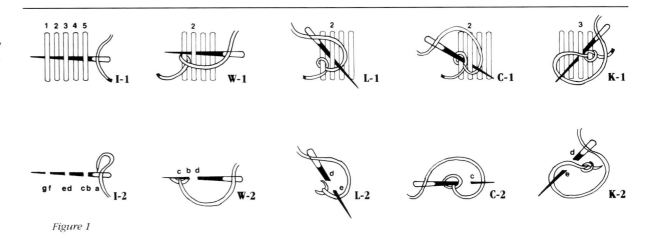

Figure 1

stitches is also useful in the analysis of antique and ancient fabrics. The identification of the basic binding unit—the stitch—gives clues to the method of construction, and a concise way to describe structure.

In spite of this rather technical introduction, the book is designed to be a hands-on guide for the craftsman. One learns five basic stitches and how they work upon different foundations to construct and accessorize fabric. I sincerely hope that the book provides practical information, inspiration, and endless hours of pleasure stitching. I worked with embroidery and needlelace for many years before I began weaving. My vocabulary of stitches was useful in many ways, from working with tapestry, textures, and openwork, to hemming and finishing. Only a few of the many stitches that will work upon warp are traditionally taught in weaving texts, and stitches in needlework books need some translation for working upon warp. I thought there was a need for a collation of universal stitches with structure as the basis for organization and inspiration.

—Nancy Arthur Hoskins

Honor the structures . . .
Those ancient laws . . .
Basic . . .
Universal . . .

Jack Lenor Larsen
"Time Was and Is"

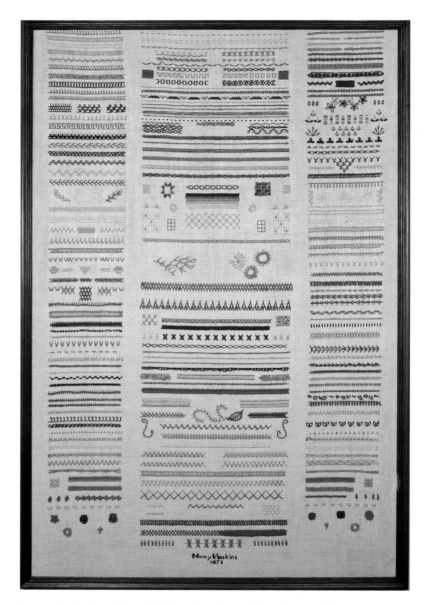

A sampler by the author of all the embroidery stitches in Jacqueline Enthoven's *The Stitches of Creative Embroidery. Photo credit: Alexis Garrett.*

PART ONE: The Learning Projects

Projects that suggest sequence, method, and materials for learning the stitches are outlined in this chapter. The sequence of stitches guides the student from the basic and universal to the complex and unique. The method of learning is the sampler. The materials which were selected for the projects work well, are inexpensive, and readily available.

The learning projects are:
1. Five Basic Stitches on Fabric
2. Five Basic Stitches on Warp
3. A Sampler of Variations and Combinations
4. A Sampler of Stitches for Edges
5. The Frame-loom Sampler
6. The Heirloom Sampler
7. The Loom Sampler

The first four projects are designed for maximum learning with a minimum investment of money and time. Process, not product, is their purpose. A very respectable repertoire of stitches will be learned in these first projects.

The frame-loom sampler is included to teach the basics of frame-loom weaving in the tapestry mode to those who are new to that technique, and to encourage combinations of interlacing, wrapping, looping, chaining, and knotting stitches in a freely designed mini-weaving.

The dedicated student will discover in Projects 6 and 7 the challenge of creating a treasured sampler upon finished fabric or as a handloomed project. Either sampler could be an in-depth study of all stitches in the book or of a selected set.

Become familiar with the section on stitches before you begin any of the projects. The first few pages of that section explain the rationale of the diagramming system used throughout the stitch index, where stitches are arranged to expedite your learning.

These first few projects may seem simplistic to those of you who are already experienced with weaving and embroidery— yet I think you will find the exercises worthwhile. Because information is presented in a new and integrated order, weavers can learn more about stitches and stitchers can learn more about weaving. I use Projects 1, 2, and 3 as the beginning lessons for my weaving classes.

If what you already know concerning terms, techniques, and traditions gets in your way, simply work it out with a sample and focus on the details of structure. "The prerequisite of originality is the art of forgetting—at the proper moment—what we know," said Arthur Koestler. An essential aspect of creative action seems to be the ability to rearrange what one knows into new formations.

I now see all fiber art in terms of structure.
Fibers, from diverse sources with inherent and indelible characteristics, are made directly into felt-like fabrics or spun into elements.
Elements—spun, plied, and dyed—are connected using various tools and processes into stitches that form fabric.

Fabric is a pliable plane that can be stitched upon, cut, pieced, and manipulated in countless creative ways to form fabrications.

To 'fabricate' implies both to build and to fantasize. But first, one must learn. You bring to all of these projects your own special interests, experiences, and imagination.

General Materials List for All Projects

☐ *SCISSORS*
-large fabric cutting shears
-small sharp snipping scissors

☐ *NEEDLES*
-no. 13 and 16 large eyed *blunt* needles
    Blunt needles are a necessity for the stitching methods you will be taught in this book.

☐ *FRAME AND FRAME-LOOM*
-14"×18" canvas stretcher or other wooden frame
    A canvas stretcher is a frame made of four pre-cut notched boards available in most art supply stores. Any sturdy wood frame of those dimensions would suffice. This frame, used in Projects 3 and 4 to mount the fabric upon, will be converted to a frame-loom for the weaving project (5) with the addition of a few simple parts.

-1/2" dowel 12" long
-2 wood blocks 1"×4"×4"
-screws or nails
    Complete instructions for making and
    warping the frame-loom are outlined in
    Project 5. Any other commercial or handmade
    frame loom, table loom, or floor loom will
    work for this woven sampler.
-tacks or staples and staple gun

☐ *FOUR-HARNESS TABLE OR FLOOR LOOM*
Project 7, The Loom Sampler, and some of the
ideas suggested in Part Three: "An Album of
Ideas" require a working knowledge of the four-
harness loom.

☐ *MEASURING TAPE OR RULER*

☐ *FORK OR TAPESTRY BEATER*

☐ *SHED SWORD, WOODEN KNITTING
    NEEDLE, OR PICK-UP STICK*

☐ *CARDBOARD*
Any cardboard firm enough to support stretched
warp threads will work.

☐ *MASKING TAPE*

☐ *BURLAP—1-1/2 YARD*
Run the burlap through the clothes dryer on an
air cycle before using to remove the excess lint.
Reserve the selvages of the cloth when cutting
the fabric for the samplers. Cut edges may be
secured with iron on facing, with zigzag
machine stitching, or with masking tape.

☐ *YARN*
-No. 3 pearl cotton
-medium weight yarns
    four ply knitting, rya, tapestry, needlepoint, or
    other yarn of a comparable size with a firmly
    twisted ply or a snug, smooth spin. These
    yarns are for the burlap samples.
-variety yarns of different weights and textures
    for the mini-weaving.
-Colors:
    Colors that relate to the structural stitch
    families are recommended for the samplers.
    Select *five* different hues to represent the *five
    stitch families.* Add at least two values, a light
    and a dark, or two analogous hues to each
    basic color. For instance, interlacing stitches
    might be all in green—pure green, light
    green, dark green, yellow-green or
    blue-green.
-Warp yarn for Project 7
    no. 3 pearl cotton or linen of choice

General Instructions for Stitching

☐ *THE STITCHING ELEMENT*
Cut a stitching element about 30" long. Don't try
to stitch with an over long thread. There is
always a way to stop and start new threads.

☐ *ATTACHING THE STITCHING ELEMENT*
On a single element or warp foundation:
    Make a temporary attachment by knotting the
    end of the stitching element to the position
    suggested in each diagram, but leave a 3" tail
    past the knot. When the project is finished the
    tail can be clipped off if the knot is incon-
    spicuous, or stitched into the back of the

fabric. In some weaves—tapestry or double
weave—the tail can be taken into the weave.
At the end of a row of stitches secure the
stitching element as neatly as possible. Slip
the needle into the weave, into the back of the
stitch, or to the back of the fabric. Sewing
thread or invisible thread can be used to
secure the stitching element at the beginning
and end of a row if knots are too bulky. The
finishing should be secure and unobtrusive.
Upon fabric:
    When working upon fabric tie a small knot on
    the end of the stitching element both at the
    beginning and the end of the row of stitches.
    If the piece requires a fine finishing on the
    back, leave a tail past the knot to be worked
    into the back of some stitches, after the knot is
    untied.

☐ *IF YOU ARE LEFT-HANDED*
All of the five basic stitches have two sets of
diagrams for constructional and accessory
stitches demonstrating how each stitch works
from left to right and also from right to left. I-1,
I-2, W-1, W-2, L-1, L-2, C-1, C-2, K-1, and K-2 illus-
trate the preferred stitch for most right-
handed stitchers. I-4, W-4, W-5, L-5, L-6, C-4, C-5,
K-4, and K-5 would be the version most comfortable for those who are left-handed. You are
encouraged to become ambidextrous.

1. *Five Basic Stitches on Fabric*

You should be completely familiar with the accessory version of the five basic stitches before proceeding to any other learning project. Complete directions and diagrams for learning the stitches are in the index section, but the following illustrations show the finished stitch.

An interlacing stitch on fabric— ◯ ◯ ◯   **I-2**

A wrapping stitch on fabric—   ꙮꙮꙮ   **W-2**

A looping stitch on fabric—   ꙮꙮꙮ   **L-2**

A chaining stitch on fabric—   ꙮꙮꙮ   **C-2**

A knotting stitch on fabric—   ꙮꙮꙮ   **K-2**

Figure 2

Stitching upon fabric, rather than upon warp, is the easiest way to begin. Fabric provides a firm foundation so that stitches stay in place and are clearly visible. The important stitching techniques for working from right to left, or left to right, setting the needle at the appropriate angle, and correctly positioning the stitching element must be mastered. The significant differences between an interlace, wrap, loop, chain, and knot should be noted. All stitch variations and combinations worked on different foundations will be easier once you are fluent with the basic five upon fabric.

□ *MATERIALS*
-burlap 12"×12" (reserve a 3" strip at each selvage)
-yarn—medium weight
-no. 13 blunt yarn needle

□ *METHODS*
Work several rows of each stitch listed below on the burlap. Learn to work the stitches from left to right and from right to left. You should be able to create each of these five stitches without looking at the diagrams after some practice.

□ *DIAGRAMS*

I-2   L-2, L-6   K-2, K-5
W-2, W-5   C-2, C-5

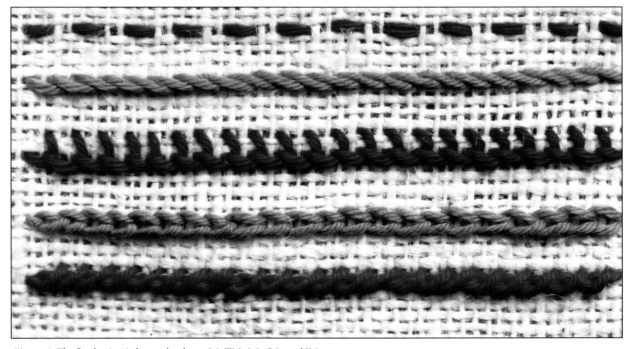

Figure 3: The five basic stitches on burlap—I-2, W-2, L-2, C-2, and K-2.

2. Five Basic Stitches on Warp

A 'loom' is any means of holding a stretched warp which has the addition of a device for lifting 'warps' for the passage of a 'weft'.[11] Looms can be very complex or extremely simple. In this instance the cardboard loom acts to hold the stretched warp and the needle lifts the warp threads for the passage of the weft. The 'warp' is the set of longitudinal elements stretched on the loom, and 'sett' is the spacing of those warp elements or 'ends'.[12] The 'weft' is the transverse element that interworks with the warp.[13]

Small samples done on cardboard with needle and yarn are useful for several reasons:
-Determining sett for any weaving project.
-Understanding the structural distinctions between different weaves—balanced plain or tabby weaves, weft-faced or tapestry weaves, warp-faced weaves, basket weaves, twill weaves, and others.
-Experimenting with the color and texture effects of various yarns.
-Learning how a stitch works on warp.

I begin every weaving project with these small samples on cardboard to discover the perfect relationship between warp and weft. My weaving students work these samples as a first weaving experience. Simply winding warps within a one inch space, as is often suggested for determining sett, does not give a complete idea of the warp and weft interrelationship.

□ *MATERIALS*
-no. 16 blunt yarn needle
-no. 3 pearl cotton (two colors)
-cardboard
There are two ways of using the cardboard strips for small samples.
Option one:
1. Cut a cardboard strip 2"×4"
2. Mark a 1" square in the center of the strip. (fig. 4)
3. Tie the warp element to the back of the cardboard.
4. Wind the warp element the specified number of times within the 1" horizontal space. The number of warps represents the number of 'ends per inch', 'e.p.i.' or sett. (fig. 5)
5. Tie the end of the warp element to the back of the cardboard.
Option two:
This method works well when the sett is not too dense; the cardboard notches are weak if cut too close together. The cardboard can be of any size and shape, the method used for many simple and creative weaving projects.
1. Cut a 2"×4" cardboard strip.
2. Mark a 1" square in the center of the strip. (fig. 4)
3. Cut notches 1/4" deep within the 1" space at the top and at the bottom of the card-

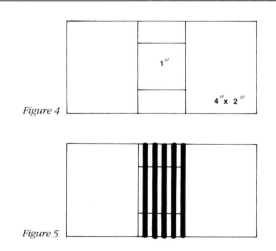

Figure 4

Figure 5

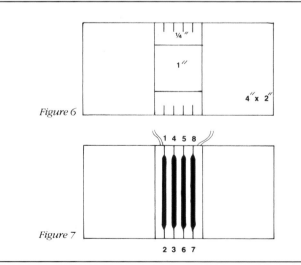

Figure 6

Figure 7

board. Cut a notch for every warp end per inch. (fig. 6)

4. Tie a knot in the end of the warp element. Slip the knot into the back of the first notch.
5. Follow the diagram (fig. 7) for winding on the warp. The warp element slips in notch 2 at the bottom, goes across the back, comes out at notch 3, goes to the top and in at notch 4, out at notch 5, etc.
6. The last warp is knotted on the back of the last notch.

□ METHODS

Sample One: Tabby or balanced plain weave (I-1, I-4)

1. Wind 12 warp ends within the 1" space for 12 e.p.i.
2. Thread the needle with the pearl cotton.
3. Follow I-1 and I-4 and work 12 rows of inter-lacing within the 1" vertical space. A row of interlacing in weaving is called a 'pick'. When warp ends and weft picks are equal within a 1" space the weave is a balanced plain weave. Different sizes of yarn would require more or less warp ends and weft picks to create a balanced cloth. A critical decision for any weaving project is how many ends and picks per inch one should use. Experiment with other weights of yarn to try to achieve a

Figure 8

balanced weave. Cut off the samples and file them for future reference.

Sample Two: Tapestry or weft-faced weave (I-6)

1. Wind 6 warp ends within the 1" space.
2. Thread the needle with the pearl cotton.
3. Work rows of interlacing until the 1" vertical space is woven.
4. Count the weft picks. Because of the spacing of the warp ends the wefts pack down, cover the warp, and create a fabric that is weft-faced. Pictorial weavings in tapestry and weft-faced pattern weaves are based on this structure. Any one pick may consist of several color changes in tapestry giving the illusion of painting.

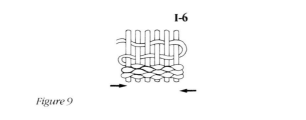

Figure 9

Sample Three: Warp-faced weave (I-7)

1. Wind two colors together 10 times around the 1" space for a total of 20 e.p.i. Keep the colors alternating—dark, light, dark, light— as they go around the cardboard.
2. Thread the needle with pearl cotton.
3. Interlace over and under the twenty ends.
4. Pull the weft firmly after each pick.
5. Use the needle to beat down the wefts. The weft will almost disappear and the warp will predominate when there are densely packed

warps. This is called a warp-faced weave. Inkle belts are the most familiar of the warp-faced weaves.

Figure 10

Sample Four: Basket weave (I-8)

1. Wind 12 warp ends within the 1" space.
2. Thread the needle with a *double strand* of pearl cotton.
3. Interlace over and under warp *pairs*. This fabric is a 2 over 2 basket weave: two wefts over two warps. It is also called an extended tabby or plain weave.

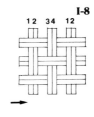

Figure 11

Sample Five: Twill weave (I-9)

1. Wind 8 ends within the 1" space. Assign each

end a number—1, 2, 3, 4, 1, 2, 3, 4. Work from the bottom to the top of the warp.
2. Thread the needle with pearl cotton.
3. Interlace the warps in this sequence.
First pick: (from right to left) over 4, under 3 & 2, over 1 & 4, under 3 & 2, over 1.
Second pick: (from left to right) under 1 & 2, over 3 & 4, under 1 & 2, over 3 & 4.
Third pick: (from right to left) under 4, over 3 & 2, under 1 & 4, over 3 & 2, under 1.
Fourth pick: (from left to right) over 1 & 2, under 3 & 4, over 1 & 2, under 3 & 4.
Interlacing in a twill sequence creates diagonal lines in the weave. Many complex patterns are derived from twill weaves.

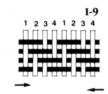

I-9

Figure 12

Sample Six: Weaving on radiating elements (I-24, I-25)
1. Tape or tie onto a cardboard *square* a set of radiating elements with a long thread.
2. Thread the end of the warp through a needle.
3. Follow the stitch instructions and stitch a knot at the center of the elements. This will make the total number of spokes uneven, and tie them together at the center.
4. Interlace over and under the set of radiating elements from the center to the outside of the

circle. Woven baskets and delicate laces are diverse examples of fabrics that use this stitch.

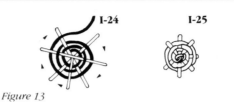

I-24   **I-25**

Figure 13

Wrapping, looping, chaining, and knotting, as well as interlacing will work upon warp to create either closely packed weft-faced areas, or if spaced, open areas. If the stitch works back and forth—that is, one pick from left to right and then one pick from right to left—the two rows of the stitch will appear countered. If instead every other row is interlaced, the same stitch angle can be maintained. Either appearance can be desirable for textural contrast.

Sample Seven: Wrapping Stitch
1. Wind 8 warp ends within the 1" space.
2. Thread the needle with the pearl cotton.
3. Follow these diagrams and work 4 picks. (W-1, W-4)

W-1

Figure 14

4. Follow these diagrams and work 4 picks. (W-1, W-6)
5. Follow these diagrams and work 4 picks. (W-1, I-1)
6. Work one row in an open area. (W-1)

Sample Eight: Looping Stitch
1. Wind 8 warp ends within the 1" space.
2. Thread the needle with pearl cotton.
3. Follow these diagrams and work 4 picks. (L-1, L-5)
4. Follow these diagrams and work 4 picks. (L-1, I-1)
5. Work one row in an open area. (L-1)

L-1

Figure 15

Sample Nine: Chaining Stitch
1. Wind 8 warp ends within the 1" space.
2. Thread the needle with the pearl cotton.
3. Follow these diagrams and work 4 picks. (C-1, C-4)
4. Follow these diagrams and work 4 picks. (C-1, I-1)
5. Work one row in an open area. (C-1)

C-1

Figure 16

Sample Ten: Knotting Stitch
1. Wind 8 warp ends within the 1" space.
2. Thread the needle with the pearl cotton.
3. Follow these diagrams and work 4 picks.
   (K-1, K-4)
4. Follow these diagrams and work 4 picks.
   (K-1, I-4)
5. Work one row in an open area. (K-1)

K-1

Figure 17

□ *DIAGRAMS*

I-1	W-1	L-1	C-1	K-1
I-4	W-4	L-5	C-4	K-4
I-6	W-6			
I-7				
I-8				
I-9				
I-24				
I-25				

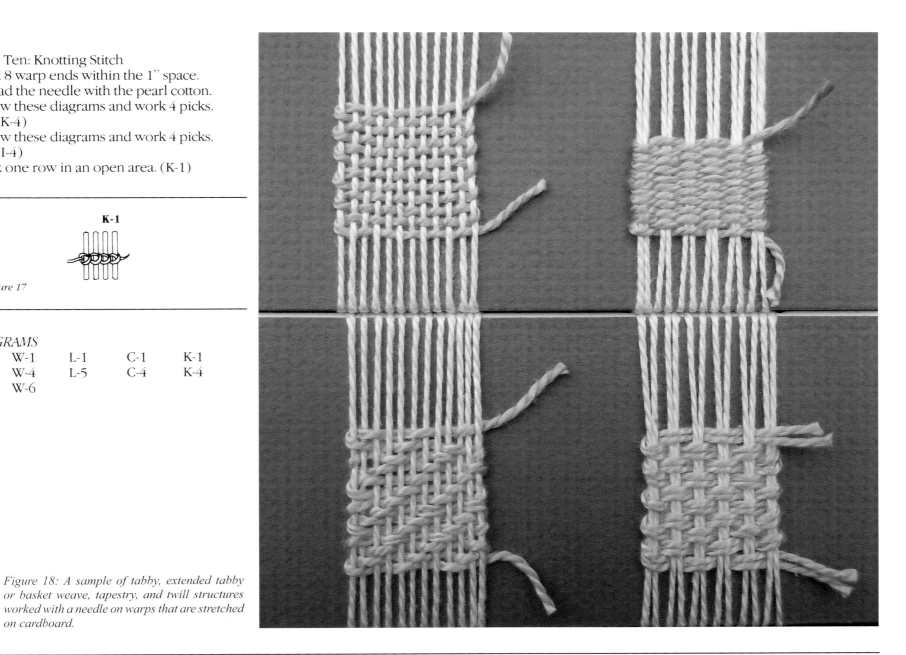

Figure 18: A sample of tabby, extended tabby or basket weave, tapestry, and twill structures worked with a needle on warps that are stretched on cardboard.

3. A Sampler of Variations and Combinations

Each of the five basic stitches will work upon:

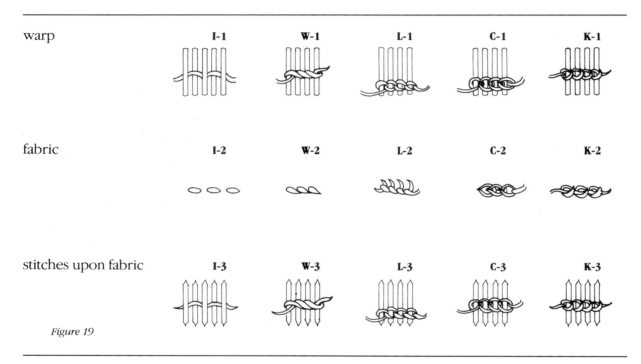

warp	I-1	W-1	L-1	C-1	K-1
fabric	I-2	W-2	L-2	C-2	K-2
stitches upon fabric	I-3	W-3	L-3	C-3	K-3

Figure 19

Some embroidery stitches, called 'bar', or 'band', or 'raised band' stitches, are made with a row or rows of stitches working upon another foundation set of parallel straight stitches. I think of these as 'superstructural stitches'; that is, one builds a superstructure of stitches on the fabric and then uses them as the foundation for other stitches. Stitches that will work upon warp can be translated to this type of accessory stitch, and vice versa. The set of stitches upon fabric simulates the warp, and the stitch works across those elements without going back into the

fabric until the end of the row. Only the basic five stitches are illustrated in all three ways—upon warp, upon fabric, and upon a set of stitches on fabric— but many others will work this way, and are so indicated in the listing of the foundations as 'stitches on fabric'. (See the chart on page 14 for the listing of band stitches for fabric edges—all of these will work upon warp or as 'superstructural stitches'.)

The first part of this project is designed to expand the stitch vocabulary by describing how the basic five stitches work upon three different foundations. The second part of the project adds a selected list of variations and combinations to the sampler. The method of working upon burlap fabric is suggested to expedite learning by simulating, with an embroidery technique, working upon a warp foundation. The Textile Museum suggests the term 'withdrawn element work' for this technique, traditionally called withdrawn thread work or drawn work.[14] Weft elements are withdrawn from the cloth and the exposed warp used as a foundation for stitches. The method described can be utilized for learning many other stitches. The three different versions of each stitch—on warp, on fabric, and upon stitches on fabric—will be aligned on the fabric in columns for comparison. (fig. 20)

□ *MATERIALS*
-frame 14"×18"
-tacks or staple gun
-no. 13 blunt yarn needle
-yarn
  medium weight
  color coded for the five stitch families
-burlap 20"×24"
  1. Press the burlap.
  2. Lay the frame on the burlap.
  3. Turn the edges of the fabric under 1".
  4. Tack or staple the fabric to the frame, begin-ning at the center of each side and working toward the corners. The fabric should be taut, but not tight. The warp and weft threads should be straight with the frame.
  5. There will be an area about 14-1/2" wide and 10-1/2" high for stitching, if one excludes the fabric that is stretched over the frame at either side. Divide this space into five columns, each about 2" wide with 1" spaces in between. The easiest way to do this is to lay a measuring tape across the 18" width and take a long stitch from 2 to 4, from 5 to 7, from 11 to 13, and from 14 to 16. (fig. 20)

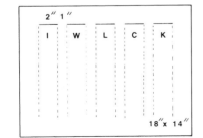

Figure 20

6. The five stitches will be arranged in columns—Interlacing, Wrapping, Looping, Chaining, Knotting.
7. To simulate how a stitch works upon warp, weft elements will be withdrawn from the 2" wide area at the top of each column. Follow these instructions for the first exposed warp area in each column.
  a. Clip 6 weft threads at the center of column one, just below the inner edge of the frame.

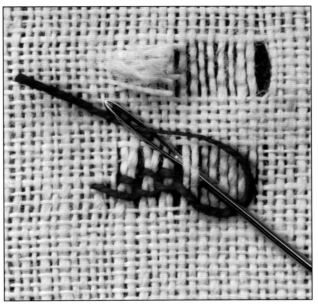

Figure 21: Weft elements are clipped and then cut away so that stitches can be worked on the exposed warps.

  b. With a needle withdraw these 6 clipped wefts within the 2" wide column, pulling them to the right and to the left. Cut them

at the edge of the column. Beauty is not the object of this lesson. Glue, a small bit of iron-on bonding tape, or masking tape can secure the cut edges. As long as the burlap is on the frame the cut threads are quite stable.
  c. Repeat this procedure at the top of each column. Follow a weft thread across so that the top of each column will be aligned.

□ *METHODS*
Column One: Interlacing Stitches
1. Begin and end all rows of stitches with a knot on the back of the fabric.
2. Work all constructional stitches upon *pairs of warps*.
3. Keep the different versions of the stitch the same size.
4. Work the constructional version of interlacing on the exposed warp. (I-1)
5. Stitch a row of the accessory version of inter-lacing about 6 weft threads below the open warp area. Work over and under pairs of threads to keep the stitches in proportion. (I-2)
6. With a second value of the color you are using for interlacing, stitch about 10 warp-wise parallel stitches across the 2" column. The top of the row should be about 6 weft threads below the last row of stitches. Make the stitches about 6 weft threads high. Keep this same spacing for all of the 'bar' stitches on the sampler. (W-14)
7. Work a row of interlacing upon the set of stitches with a different color. (I-3)
8. Observe the three versions of interlacing

upon warp, upon fabric, and upon a foundation of stitches.

Follow the above procedure for the three versions of the other four basic stitches in column two, three, four, and five. The diagram numbers are listed in the diagram chart. Use a different color for each stitch column.

The essential structure of a stitch does not change even though the foundation varies. The active stitching element works over or around a warp or a portion of fabric in a characteristic pattern. The same structure might be formed with a needle, butterfly, shuttle, or other tool.

The same stitch could work upon a metal ring, leather, or other exotic foundation. Stitch structure can still be identified.

A small set of variations and combinations, along with the basic five are fundamental to the fiber arts. I think of these as the 'common core' stitches. The common core stitches include those that are and have been universally used to construct fabric throughout the history of civilization. Each of these common core stitches is associated with a particular technique—basketry, netting, lace, knitting, and knotting, as well as weaving and embroidery. They are

significant as the prime stitch in certain ethnic fabrics and historical techniques from ancient China, Egypt, or Peru. The stitches are used in many different constructional and accessory crafts and have multiple names. The stitches suggested in this second part of Project 3 include all of these common core stitches plus a few personal favorites like the stitches on radiating elements—'spider webs'.

Follow the order of the diagrams as listed in the following chart. Some stitch columns contain more stitches than others. Spaces in the shorter columns can be filled with some stitched designs or patterns, or with other stitches added from the stitch index.

☐ DIAGRAMS

Interlacing Column 1	Wrapping Column 2	Looping Column 3	Chaining Column 4	Knotting Column 5
I-1	W-1	L-1	C-1	K-1
I-2	W-2	L-2	C-2	K-2
I-3	W-3	L-3	C-3	K-3
I-14	W-9	L-8	C-8	K-7
I-22	W-10	L-9	C-9	K-25
I-25	W-15	L-10	C-11	K-26
	W-16	L-11	C-12	K-37
	W-18	L-13	C-13	
	W-21	L-20		
	W-22	L-21		
	W-30	L-33		
	W-33	L-34		
	W-34	L-35		
	W-35	L-56		
	W-36			
	W-67			
	W-68			
	W-69			

Figure 22: A sampler of stitches worked on burlap with pearl and broder cottons for Project 3.

Distinctive finishes on handwoven products require an interesting vocabulary of stitches. Stitches that create functional and decorative edges on selvages, folds, warp hems, or between two pieces of fabric are based on the basic five, and certain variations and combinations. Often the same stitch will work in several ways.

Some stitches for edges make a single row and work over and under the edge of the fabric. Purely decorative accessory stitches, as opposed to these functional stitches that actually work with the edge are not listed in the diagram chart, but you will discover many of these in the stitch index. Just experiment.

Lace edges, similar to those done with crochet or tatting, can be worked with the needlelace stitches. A lace edge can also be used as a wide join by stitching the bottom row of the lace onto the second fabric. (fig. 25)

A few stitches for fringes and picots (stitched rings) are included in the list of diagrams.

The frame will again be used for holding the fabric for this sampler, but the fabric will be arranged in strips so that stitches can be practiced on edges and between edges.

☐ *MATERIALS*
-frame 14"×18"
-yarn
 medium weight

colors coded for stitch families
-burlap strips
1. Cut 18" strips of burlap 3" wide from each selvage.
2. Arrange these strips as illustrated in fig. 23.
3. Turn the raw edge under and place the strips so that there are folds next to folds, selvages next to selvages, and wide and narrow spaces in between.
4. Tack or staple the strips to the frame across the 14" span.
5. Cut one 22" strip (this does not need a selvage) turn the raw edge, and attach this strip cross the 18" bottom part of the frame. Withdraw the weft elements from the unattached edge.

The parallel strips with selvages and folds can be used for practicing stitches on one or between

two edges. The bottom strip with the warp fringe can be used to practice hemming stitches. This is rather an odd looking sampler, but very functional for our purposes.

☐ *METHODS*
Foundations are differentiated in the diagram pages as:

fabric edge   fabric edges

warp and woven fabric

Figure 24

Lace edges can be stitched down to the second fabric edge to join two pieces of fabric.

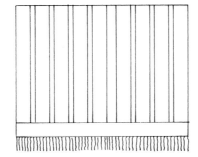

Figure 23

W-21   **L-10**   **W-52**

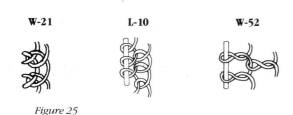

Figure 25

Many of the stitches that will work across a set of warp or work upon a set of foundation stitches can be used to join two pieces of fabric. Just stitch one set of parallel straight stitches to the fabric pieces and then embellish those foundation stitches with another stitch. If you will turn the diagrams 90 degrees you will see how those can work. The following chart lists the band or bar stitches that will work in this fashion.

L-8   **W-33**

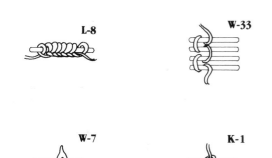

W-7   **K-1**

Figure 26

□ *DIAGRAMS*

Fabric Edge	Fabric Edges	Band Stitches for Edges	Warp and Woven Fabric
W-11	I-22	I-3	I-14
W-18 (lace)	W-23	I-6	W-49
W-27	W-25	I-10	L-7
W-36 (fringe)	W-31	I-14	L-55
W-48 (fringe)	W-32	I-22	C-6
W-52 (lace)	W-41	W-3	C-10
W-54	W-44	W-7	K-6
L-4	W-47	W-9	K-18
L-9 (lace)	W-56	W-15	K-29
L-10 (lace)	L-19	W-30	
L-11 (lace)	L-22	W-33	
L-13 (lace)	L-27	W-42	
L-16	L-30	W-45	
L-35 (lace)	L-39	W-50	
L-36	L-42	L-3	
L-43	L-49	L-5	
L-45 (lace)	L-50	L-20	
L-50 (picot)	L-51	L-25	
L-51 (picot)	K-9	L-28	
L-52 (lace)	K-12	L-31	
L-54 (lace)	K-23	L-32	
K-11	K-28	L-40	
K-22	K-31	L-46	
K-34 (fringe)	K-32	L-50	
		L-51	
		C-3	
		C-4	
		C-11	
		K-3	
		K-6	
		K-24	
		K-25	

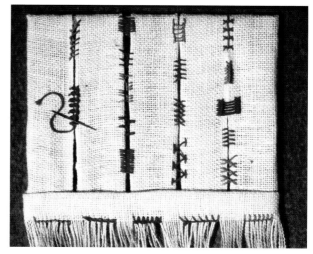

Figure 27: A sampler of stitches for edges and hems worked on burlap strips for Project 4.

Unique combinations of interlacing, wrapping, looping, chaining and knotting are possible within the tapestry mode. With the weft-faced plain weave structure as a starting point, explore the design possibilities of the different stitches. Translate the stitching skill acquired upon the fabric and cardboard supports to the warp.

Designing is always a problem when trying out some new skill. How do you learn without designing? How can you design effectively without knowing all aspects of the structure? Set some limits whenever approaching a new skill—a new structure. Limit the size of the piece, limit the materials, limit the colors, but experiment and explore how stitches can create different surface textures, openwork areas, high relief, pile or lace effects. Discover how certain stitches can span spaces, overlay areas, or move off of the woven plane. Do not try to work with a preconceived composition, but let the mini-weaving grow stitch by stitch, row by row. Work with the needle, work with the butterfly, or work with a shuttle—whatever works best.

□ *MATERIALS*
-no. 13 and 16 blunt yarn needles
-fork or tapestry beater
-string
-yarns
    warp: no. 3 pearl cotton, 25 yards,

6 e.p.i.×6" wide=36 ends, color coordinated with the weft yarns.

weft: Select a combination of colors, weights, and textures that harmonize with the warp. Your final selection should have one dominant color in greater quantity, varied hues, values, textures, and weights of your selected colors, and accent colors in small quantities. Select some yarns that will stitch well, but also those that present interesting problems because of their fuzziness or unusual construction. (See couching, p. 42) The weft yarns can be threaded through a needle or used in small wound hanks of yarn called 'butterflies' for interworking with the warp. Use whatever method is most expedient for the stitch that you are using. If you are working several rows of interlacing, a butterfly will work well, but if you change to a looping, knotting, or other complex stitch a threaded needle may work best. If you are working the mini-weaving upon a table or floor loom there may be times when a shuttle should be used.

-butterfly
1. Use the thumb and the little finger of your left hand.
2. Wind the weft yarn in a figure '8' pattern between the thumb and little finger.
3. Grasp the center of the yarn hank where the threads cross, and slip the yarn off your hand.

4. Wind the working end of the yarn several times around the center cross, and secure that end with a looping stitch.
5. Pull from the starting end to use the butterfly.

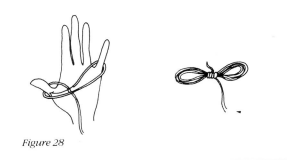

Figure 28

-frame-loom
1. Assembling the frame-loom
The following diagram illustrates the parts of the frame-loom. The blocks and dowel that make the 'heddle bar' will not be mounted onto the frame until after the warp is on, but if you are going to drill the screw holes do so *before* warping.

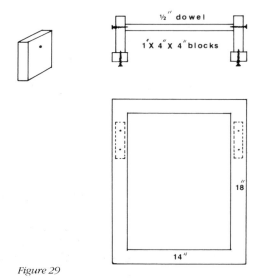

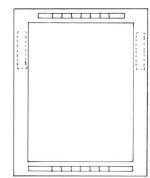

Figure 30

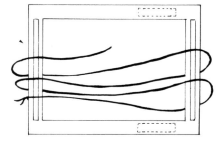

Figure 31

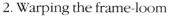

Figure 29

e. The warp needs to be taut, but not tight. Begin at one edge of the warp and pull each warp in turn to take up the slack. Retie at the opposite end.

f. Use a bit of tape to keep the first and last warp at either side in their correct position either at the front or at the back of the frame.

g. Cut a 24" string. Slip this string in the open 'shed' between the two layers of warp at the top of the loom. (fig. 33) Bring the string to the bottom as far as it will go and tie it to the frame at both sides. This will be the bottom edge of your weaving.

h. Begin at the middle warps and work to either edge spacing the six warps between each inch mark, as they intersect the horizontal holding string.

i. Space the warps at the top of the loom so that they are parallel.

j. Run a strip of masking tape across the bottom of the frame to keep the spaced warps in position.

k. Nail or screw the dowel to the wooden blocks.

l. Nail or screw the blocks to the frame.

m. Cut 18 strings 14" long.

n. Each string must pass around a warp that is coming off the *back* of the frame near the top of the loom, and then be tied to the heddle bar. This is a 'string heddle'. The string heddles will pull a set of warps forward for the passage of the weft. It is very important that each string heddle is in the space between the two warps that come off the front of the loom. (fig. 32)

2. Warping the frame-loom
   a. Put a strip of masking tape across the top and the bottom of the loom. Mark the center of the 14" sides on the tape. Mark each inch, three inches to the right of center and three inches to the left of center. (fig. 30)

   b. Turn the frame sideways. Tie the end of the warp thread at the three inch mark on the lower left side. Wind the warp onto the frame with a figure '8' pattern (fig. 31) until 18 warps show across the tape. They should be spaced so that three warps show between every inch.

   c. Tie the warp at the three inch mark on the upper left side.

   d. There should be a *total* number of 36 warp ends. Remember only half of them show across the front of the frame, the other half are coming across the back. Look at the warp from the side to see if the warps are accurately crossed. The system will not work unless the warps are in order.

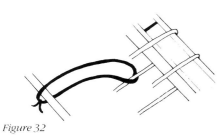

Figure 32

o. Prop the frame-loom against a table edge or wall for the working position.

☐ *METHODS*
Weaving on the frame-loom
1. Slip a 1"×7" cardboard strip in the space between the holding string and the frame. This will give you an even weft line to beat against as you begin weaving.
2. Begin the frame loom sampler with a 1" heading of weft-faced plain weave in your dominant color.
3. Working rows of interlacing from right to left.
   a. Begin at the right edge of the warp.
   b. Slip the butterfly of yarn in the open shed formed by the two layers of warp. (fig. 34) Shed 1 is the open shed.
   c. Bring the weft yarn to the left edge of the warp.
   d. Do not pull the weft yarn straight across between the warps, but allow for some slack and softness.
   e. Use the fork to beat the weft against the holding string.
   f. Wrap the weft around the warp end at the left edge.

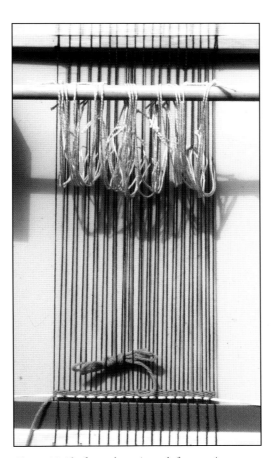

Figure 33: The frame-loom is ready for weaving.

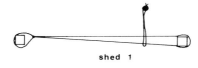

shed 1

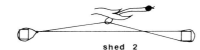

shed 2

Figure 34

4. Working rows of interlacing from left to right.
   a. Working with a set of three or four warps at a time, pull on the string heddles to open a shed. Hold the shed open with your fingers and slip the butterfly through the shed. (fig. 34) Shed 2 is the one that is pulled open. Repeat this sequence of actions across the warp.
   b. Beat the weft down. Remember to allow some slack.
   c. Wrap the weft around the warp end at the right edge.
5. Repeat steps 3 and 4 whenever rows of plain interlacing are wanted.
6. Colors and yarns may be changed at any intersection of warp and weft, except at the edges. Let the end of the new color and the clipped end of the color just used dangle to the back of the weaving. Subsequent beating in of other rows will secure the ends.
7. Stitches may change at any intersection of warp and weft. This is your opportunity to be experimental with solidly stitched weft-faced areas or with unusual openwork areas. Look through the stitch diagrams and at your other samples for ideas.
8. Strive to keep the weft wraps at the edges even. Each change of yarn, stitch, or tension will alter an even edge unless you accommodate for them. Constant vigilance is the secret to well crafted edges. Measure and maintain the width of the weaving established in the first few picks.
9. *Before* cutting the weaving off the frame-loom, stitch a row of knotting stitches at the top and at the bottom between the holding string and the first pick.

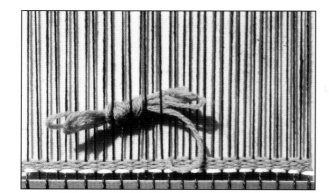

Figure 35: The butterfly slips in the open shed from right to left.

Figure 36: The fingers hold open the second shed so that the butterfly can be interlaced from left to right.

Figure 37: "From My Garden" by Genie Langdon, a University of Oregon student, was done on a frame-loom. Textural interest was created both with stitches and with variety yarns. 10"×14"

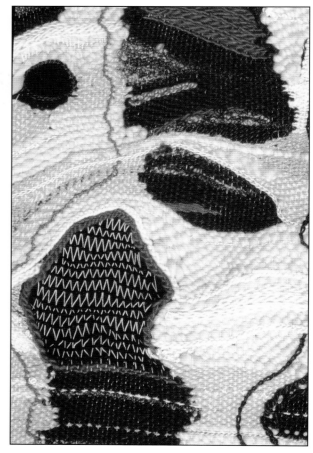

Figure 38: "De Beque Canyon" by Ardis Letey was created during a workshop on tapestry and embroidery stitches for the Eugene Stitchery Guild. The detail of the tapestry shows how a variety of stitches define, outline, and enrich the plain weave areas.

□ DIAGRAMS

The diagram numbers listed below are either traditional or historical tapestry techniques. Try these, but remember that many other stitches will work upon warp. See the chart in "Part Two: 10. Weft-faced Effects" for other stitch numbers.

I-6	W-6	W-58
I-11	W-9	W-59
I-12	W-15	W-60
W-1	W-30	W-61
W-4	W-35	

6. *An Heirloom Sampler*

"When this you see, remember me . . ."
An Old Sampler Verse

Figure 39: An English sampler done in 1834 by Harriet Knaples, age 11.

A well designed sampler is a treasure—decorative and useful forever as a reference of stitches. I have several samplers that I have done over the years on display in my home. I am as proud of those samplers as of any handwork that I have done, for each one represents a period of study and learning. I take pleasure in the fine even weave fabrics, the warm colors, and the unpretentious design. The composition of the samplers is basically symmetrical, but always with a few surprises.

The sampler that I created for this project was on a piece of Willamette Valley linen. At one time the Willamette Valley in Oregon grew linen as lovely and lustrous as any I have ever seen. The fabric is not unlike some of the 1500 year old Coptic linens that I have examined, and has the same creamy color and handle. I have a few precious yards of this fabric woven from some of the last of that Oregon flax by the late Ruth B. Wheeler. The textile has the signature of an experienced craftsman—a sure and true tabby. I used a columnar plan for the sampler composition, and a rainbow palette from green to orange of pearl and broder cottons for the stitches. All constructional versions of stitches were worked as band stitches rather than withdrawing weft elements. Stitches for edges and hems were omitted.

The disciplined student who creates a well crafted sampler will be rewarded with enriched skills. Choose harmonized colors in the finest

stitching threads and the best fabric that you can afford. Be sure to sign and date your sampler so that you will always be remembered.

□ *MATERIALS*
-no. 16 blunt needle
-frame (optional)
-fabric
　Use a balanced plain weave or basket weave textile in linen, cotton, silk, or wool. Shop for the sampler fabric with a needle in hand to test the density of the weave. The needle should slip easily through the weave without splitting the elements. The fabric should have some body and substance. 'Aida cloth' is a traditional cotton sampler cloth sold in needlework shops. Weavers can, of course, design their own sampler fabric.
-yarns
　DMC no. 3, 5, or 8 pearl cotton
　DMC Retors a broder (a matte finish cotton thread)
　tapestry yarn
　Persian yarn
　needlepoint yarn
　silk
　linen

□ *METHODS*
　1. Select the dimensions of the finished piece.
　2. Hem the edges or stretch the fabric on a frame, temporarily or permanently.

3. Choose the stitches that you plan to include in the sampler.
4. Divide the stitches into their structural families or into other logical groupings.
5. Sketch—very freely—on a paper the size of your sampler how you might divide the space, and how the stitches will fit into that space.
6. Experiment on the fabric to find the ideal size for the stitches, and the spacing between rows, then plan the spaces around that module.
7. Plan for contrasting areas. Use stitches in regular rows and also use stitches to draw and design in other areas.
8. Consider a theme or motif harmonized with the color scheme.
9. Will elements be withdrawn for rows of constructional stitches or will those be worked upon a superstructure of straight stitches?
10. Color key the stitch families.
11. *Before beginning* plan how the sampler will be finished and mounted for display.
12. *Do not draw on the fabric.* If you need guide lines, stitch them on with sewing thread that can be removed. Use cutout paper shapes pinned onto the fabric for outlines.
13. *Record* on the sampler backing fabric with iron on tape or a laundry pen the diagram numbers for each stitch.

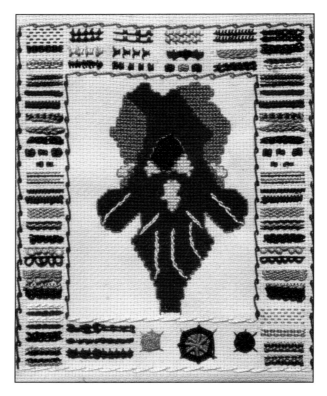

Figure 40: A sampler on Aida cloth created by Genie Langdon, a University of Oregon student in the summer of 1981.

7. A Loom Sampler

The 'samp cloth' and the 'gamp' are traditional ways of recording stitches and weaves. Though literary references appear as early as 1502, the earliest European and American sewn samplers are from the seventeenth century and show examples of floral and border patterns, lace techniques, withdrawn element work, joining stitches, and only slightly later alphabets, verse, signatures, and dates. The sampler format, a long narrow strip of linen, was dictated by the narrow loom common at that time.[15] Pre-Columbian Peruvian samplers of woven patterns and structures have also survived as a source of inspiration for our time. A loom sampler that combines constructional and accessory stitches with their variations and combinations might become a new tradition for the fiber artist of the 80's.

The loom sampler outlined in this project is planned for a straight draw threading (1, 2, 3, 4) on a four-harness loom. However, it is possible to work the sampler, with some alterations, on any two-harness system. The experienced weaver could design the sampler around any weave structure that has a tabby option. As with the heirloom sampler, color coding helps to organize the information for future reference.

□ MATERIALS
-no. 16 blunt needle
-shuttle
-knitting needle, shed sword, or pick-up stick
-four-harness loom
-yarn
    warp:
    no. 3 pearl cotton, 12 e.p.i., ecru or white linen, sleyed for tabby, natural or white
    weft:
    ground weft: same as warp
    supplementary wefts: no. 3 pearl cotton, color coded for families

□ METHODS
The sampler is designed to be divided into five separate strips after completion. The sequence of stitches follows the stitch index, and enough warp length is allowed for all stitches. Because the families contain differing numbers of variations and combinations, the individual samplers are of very different lengths. The longest sampler, the wrapping stitch family, could be divided into two pieces, closely related stitches doubled up into some areas, or only a selected set used. A shorter sampler, like the chaining family, could be balanced with a woven tabby area for accessory stitching with motifs. Sketch out some ideas on paper and consider how the samplers will be finished and mounted for display before beginning.

Figures 41, 42, 43 and 44 suggest how an area might be arranged to accommodate different foundations of open warp and woven fabric. The numbers in figures 41 and 42 represent the number of picks, the 'L' and heavy lines represent rows of looping stitches. The 6 picks of tabby and tapestry at the top and at the bottom of the diagram form borders between stitch variations. Once a module is planned it can be repeated throughout the sampler. Stitches that work warpwise, or between edges can be arranged as in fig. 42. Select a hemming stitch to be used whenever starting or stopping a

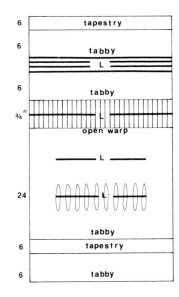

Figure 41

sampler section. Follow a consistent color plan. Because the sampler has so many open warp areas you must solve the problem of the weft picks sliding out of position and into the open areas. Here are three suggestions to keep those wefts in place.

1. Follow the diagram for the reversed knotting stitch for the wefts above and below the open warp area. (K-6)
2. Use sewing thread the same color as your warp and weft and stitch a row of knotting stitches above and below the tabby wefts in the open area. (K-1)
3. Use the twining stitch with one ground weft and the second weft of sewing thread the color of the warp and weft.(I-14)

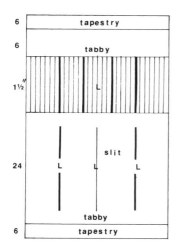

Figure 42

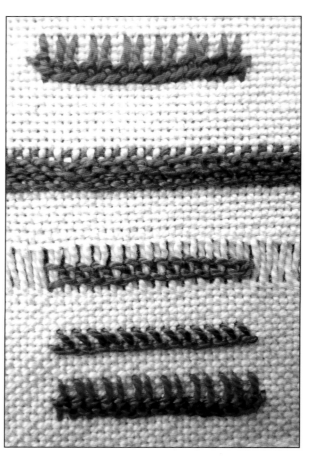

Figure 43: A detail from the loom sampler showing looping stitches worked on warp, on fabric, and upon laid stitches. The wefts above and below the open warp areas are held with a row of twining worked with the ground weft and sewing thread.

Figure 44: Slits in the tabby area are stitched together with alternating looping stitches, and those same stitches worked on the open warp areas.

□ *DRAFT*

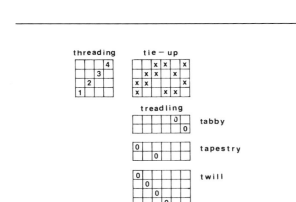

threading
tie-up
treadling

tabby

tapestry

twill

Figure 45

Width at reed 6"
Total Warp length 7 yards
   loom waste allowance 2'
   fringe allowance 5'=6"+6"×5
   stitch family sections 14'
      interlacing 2'
      wrapping 5'
      looping 4'
      chaining 1'
      knotting 2'

□ *DIRECTIONS*

Complete directions are given for only the first section of the sampler on interlacing stitches. This clearly demonstrates how a similar plan can be followed for each family section.
1. Review the suggestions for designing a sampler in Project 6.
2. Dress the loom.

3. Follow the weaving and stitching sequence that is outlined next. Unless specified the weave or stitch is done with the ground weft.

Figure 46: One set of warp threads are raised for ease of stitching.

DIRECTIONS	TOOL	WEAVE	DIAGRAM
1. Leave an 18" tail on the first weft at the right edge of the warp. 6 picks of tabby.	shuttle	tabby	I-1, I-4
2. Stitch a row of knotting stitches below the first needle row of tabby with the long weft tail.	needle		K-1
3. 6 picks of tapestry		tapestry	I-6
4. 24 picks of tabby		tabby	
5. Reserve 3/4" of open warp			
6. 6 picks of tabby			
7. 6 picks of tapestry		tapestry	

DIRECTIONS	TOOL	WEAVE	DIAGRAM
8. Work the stitch across the middle of the open warp area with a colored element.	needle		I-1
9. Work a row of interlacing stitches on the woven fabric area of 24 picks, 6 wefts down from the open area.			I-2
10. Stitch a set of warp-wise foundation stitches, 6 wefts down from the last row of stitches, then work a row of interlacing stitches upon them. (fig. 41)			I-3
11. 6 picks of tabby	shuttle	tabby	

DIRECTIONS	TOOL	WEAVE	DIAGRAM
12. 6 picks of tabby with colored weft			I-5
13. 6 picks of tabby			
14. 6 picks of tapestry with colored weft		tapestry	I-6
15. 6 picks of tabby		tabby	
16. 6 picks of basket weave with doubled strands of colored weft		tapestry	I-8
17. 6 picks of tabby		tabby	
18. 12 picks of twill with colored weft		twill	I-9
19. 6 picks of tabby		tabby	
20. Reserve 1-1/2" of open warp			
21. 6 picks of tabby			
22. Work the 'Spanish lace' stitch on the open warp area with colored weft.	needle		I-10
23. 6 picks of tabby	shuttle		
24. 6 picks of tapestry		tapestry	
25. 6 picks of tabby		tabby	
26. Work alternate rows of interlacing and interlacing with weft-loops 3 × with colored wefts single or doubled.	needle		I-13
27. 6 picks of tabby	shuttle		
28. 6 picks of tapestry		tapestry	
29. 6 picks of tabby		tabby	
30. Raise the next tabby shed, set in a colored weft, use the beater to straighten, but do not beat to the fell line.			
31. Use the needle with another color of thread and work the twining stitch.	needle		I-14
32. Beat in softly.			
33. 6 picks of tabby	shuttle	tabby	
34. With two colors of weft work twill twining.	needle	twill	I-15
35. 6 picks of tabby	shuttle	tabby	
36. 6 picks of tapestry		tapestry	
37. 6 picks of tabby		tabby	
38. Work a 'Danish medallion'	needle		I-16
39. 6 picks of tabby	shuttle		
40. Follow the knotted variation for tying the woven areas.	needle		I-17
41. 6 picks of tabby	shuttle	tabby	
42. 6 picks of tapestry		tapestry	
43. 6 picks of tabby		tabby	
44. 1 pick with a colored weft for weft floats set in on a single harness lift		harness 2	
45. 6 picks of tabby		tabby	
46. 1 pick of a colored weft for weft floats		harness 2	
47. 6 picks of tabby		tabby	
48. 1 pick of a colored weft for weft floats		harness 2	

DIRECTIONS	TOOL	WEAVE	DIAGRAM
49. 6 picks of tabby		tabby	
50. Use the first row of weft floats for—	needle		I-18, L-1
51. Use the second row of weft floats for—			I-19, L-33
52. Use the third row of weft floats for—			I-20
53. 1 pick with colored weft floats/ 1 tabby — 3 ×	shuttle	harness 2	
54. Use the three rows of weft floats for—	needle		I-21
55. 6 picks of tabby	shuttle	tabby	
56. 6 picks of tapestry		tapestry	
57. 6 picks of tabby		tabby	
58. Work a row of gauze with a colored weft. A pick-up stick, shed sword, or knitting needle could be used to hold all of the crossed warps. Raise harness 1 & 3. Go under warp 3 from the left and pick up warp 4 on the stick. Go under warp 1 from the left, and pick up warp 2 on the stick. Repeat across the warp.	needle		I-22
59. 6 picks of tabby	shuttle	tabby	
60. Work a row of gauze, 1 tabby — 3 ×			I-22
61. Use the crossed warps for interlacing	needle		I-23
62. 6 picks of tabby	shuttle	tabby	

DIRECTIONS	TOOL	WEAVE	DIAGRAM
63. 6 picks of tapestry		tapestry	
64. 24 picks of tabby		tabby	
65. Use the 24 pick woven area as a foundation for an interlaced spider web.	needle		I-25
66. 6 picks of tapestry	shuttle	tapestry	
67. 6 picks of tabby		tabby	
68. Finish the interlacing sampler with a row of knotting stitches.	needle		K-1

Follow the same general plan for the other sampler sections. Weave the 6 pick tabby and 6 pick tapestry areas as borders and separations, the open warp and 24 pick areas for stitch samples. You will need slits for samples of stitches that join two edges in the other families. Work with two butterflies or shuttles in a 24 pick area as in fig. 42.

A loom sampler could be designed around another format. By selecting a set of coordinated stitches, a columnar plan, like Project 3's, could be followed: the open warp and woven areas to work across the entire width of the piece for five different stitches. Stitches that edge and join could be the focus of a sampler on a spaced warp. A draft that is threaded and treadled for warp and weft floats could weave fabric for stitches that work upon a foundation of stitches. There are many options.

Once you have learned to work at the loom with the needle and with a variety of stitches your 'weaver-controlled' choices will be greatly multiplied.

Ancient Peruvian textile fragments are re-fashioned for the hair and clothing on these modern pillow-mounted dolls.

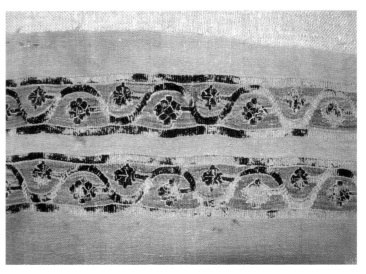

A cuff band from a Coptic Egyptian tunic has bands of wool tapestry on the linen tabby. Linen wrapping stitches embellish the leaves and grape clusters. (W-60)

Decorative tabs on a Peruvian fragment are worked with a wrapping stitch or "knit-stem stitch." (W-21)

A central roundel with a portrait has a border of dark frames with foliate motifs and a smaller portrait. The features on the faces and the warp-wise edge of the frames are defined with wrapping stitches done while weaving the tapestry. (W-60)

Plate 1: *A pensive 'Eros', from 4th Century Coptic Egypt, gazes across the centuries. The polychrome wool weft-loops on linen —now slightly frayed— are used to paint the facial features and the surrounding decorative lozenge and leaf motifs. (I-13) A detail from a 13" octagonal panel from the Metropolitan Museum of Art, Gift of George B. Pratt, 1926 (26-24-15).*

Plate 2: *A ferocious, but benevolent five-clawed dragon is beautifully detailed with minute gold wrapping wefts (W-59) and slits (I-11) dividing the colored silk and gold design areas in this 2"×3" detail from a k'o-ssu fragment (circa Ch'ing Dynasty China).*

Plate 3: *A necklace-size ceremonial circlet of birds and flowers in colorful alpaca resembles a knit fabric, but is worked with a needlelace variation of the basic wrapping stitch (W-21). This is a Peruvian, Nazca Culture (circa 0-200 A.D.) artifact from the Seattle Art Museum's Eugene Fuller Memorial Collection. (50.137) Photo Credit: Paul M. Macapia*

Plate 4: *Wrapped roundels, tassels, and bird-like tapestry figures on gauze weave are shown in a detail from a 33"×8" Peruvian shirt panel. Cochineal dyed alpaca dominates the color scheme and enhances the rhythmical fabric. Seattle Art Museum, Gift of Jack Lenor Larsen and Chan Khan, circa 1000-1470 A.D. Peruvian Chimu Culture. (69.129) Photo Credit: Paul M. Macapia*

Plate 5: *"Crescent Lake", a 4' × 10' landscape tapestry, is exhibited at the Umpqua Community College Art Gallery along with several smaller tapestries visible on the back wall— "Cascade", "Summer Solstice", "Oregon Spring" and others by Nancy Arthur Hoskins. The tree in the foreground is embellished with accessory stitches. The tapestry hangs at the Family Practice Clinic, Eugene Oregon.*

Plate 6: *A tree-branch detail from the "Crescent Lake" tapestry shows how surface stitching can enhance a tapestry weave. (L-21) Wool warp and weft, woven on an upright Barbara IV Thought Products Loom.*

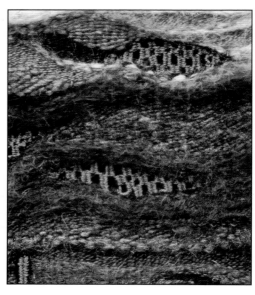

Plate 7: *"Cascade" . . . The turquoise openwork sections are worked with an alternating wrapping stitch (W-30) on warp areas that have been outlined and reserved with rows of knotting stitches. Linen warp, wool, mohair, pearl cotton wefts, woven on a frame-loom.*

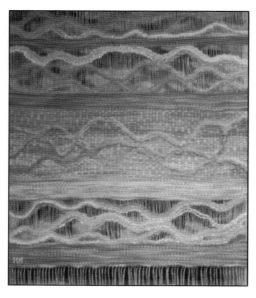

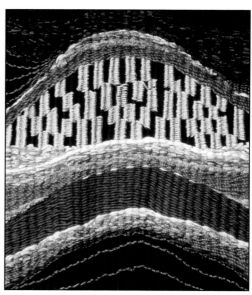

Plate 8: *"Summer Solstice" . . . Couching with invisible thread is used to add surface elements to the tapestry woven center section, and to hold the eccentric wefts in place in the openwork areas. Linen warp, onion-skin dyed wool wefts, loom woven. First publication Interweave, Summer '80.*

A detail from "The Living Waters" tapestry triptych, designed and woven by the author for the chapel at Sacred Heart Hospital in Eugene, Oregon, shows eccentric wefts and stitched open areas. (W-30, K-1)

Plate 11: "When the Vine Maple Turns" is a 9' × 17' brocaded wall hanging that hangs at the Forrest Inn, Creswell, Oregon. The highest key color areas are stitched (K-25) to add relief and emphasis. Wool warp, wool, cotton, silk, and variety wefts, loom woven in one piece. Photo Credit: Oscar Palmquist. First publication Shuttle Spindle and Dyepot, Winter '81.

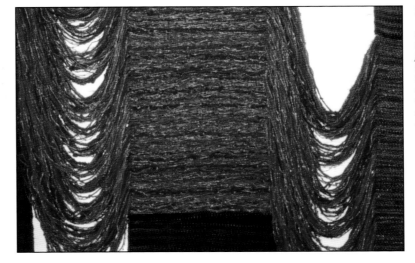

Plate 12: A detail of "Denouement" shows how the brocading wefts are knotted across the center panel and draped areas (K-1), but simply brocaded on the side panels to symbolize the knotting of a dramatic plot in Act II. Photo Credit: Oscar Palmquist

Plate 10: "Denouement" is a 6' × 12' three paneled brocaded and knotted tapestry that hangs in the Lane Community College Performing Arts Department. Cotton warp, wool and variety wefts, loom woven. Photo Credit: Oscar Palmquist

Photo credit: Alexis Garrett.

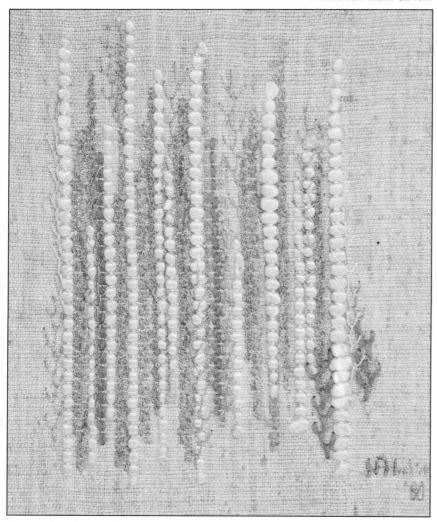

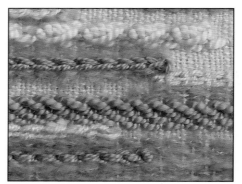

Plate 14: *"Sampler on Silk" shows how a variety of stitches worked on raised sets of warp threads will overlay the ground weave to create unusual effects. From the collection of Dr. and Mrs. George Hanson. First publication* Shuttle Spindle and Dyepot, *Winter '81.*

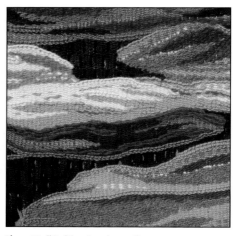

Plate 15: *"Golden Landscape" was woven on a frame-loom during a workshop taught by the author for the Eugene Stitchery Guild. Evocative of newly harvested wheat and fallow fields, artist Pam Stout skillfully contrasts and controls weft-wise stitches and openwork areas with a warm autumnal color scheme.*

Plate 16: *"Snow White" by versatile California fiber artist Helen Richards was loom woven and then embellished with a mandala that is carefully coordinated—color, texture, and yarns—with the ground fabric. Needlelace stitches were used to work the 3-D cup-like forms at the center of interest. Photo Credit: Helen Richards.*

Plate 13: *"Joey's Garden" is a brocaded and stitched tussah silk piece woven with a Moorman threading. Alternating looping stitches (I-21) are worked with the same yarns used as supplementary brocading wefts—sometimes on top of brocading wefts—for integration of design. Tussah silk warp and wefts, silk roving, pearl cottons, variety yarns, loom woven. From the collection of Dr. and Mrs. Wesley Hoskins. First publication* Shuttle Spindle and Dyepot, *Winter '81.*

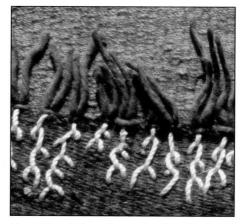

Detail from "Grass Roots" by Alda Vinson. A tapestry with surface stitching to emphasize the roots and sprouting grass. (L-21, W-36) 1976, 3' x 4', wool, linen warp.

PART TWO: An Album of Ideas

Despite the fragility of fiber, amazing art fabrics have been discovered in the necropolis sites of ancient Egypt, China, and Peru. Grave goods of silk robes, tapestry decorated linen tunics, gauze weave cotton ponchos, and lace ceremonial mantles of alpaca were buried with the dead in long forgotten rituals to provide for the life to come. Hieroglyphics from Tutankhamen's tomb translate, "To speak the name of the dead is to make them live again." The artisans from these ancient cultures live because their work is remembered and revered.

The Egyptian weaving tradition reaches five thousand years back into the time of the early Pharaohs. The descendants of the people of the Pharonic period are the Christianized Egyptians, the Copts. The Coptic Church, organized in 190 A.D. has a present day membership of six million and carries on the language, liturgy, and music of that early church. Egypt, conquered by Alexander the Great in 326 B.C., and by Rome in 30 B.C., has been an Islamic nation since 641 A.D. Tapestry techniques and classical tastes in style came with the Greco-Roman culture and flourished during the Coptic period. There are over a hundred thousand Coptic fabrics. The most interesting are the small tapestry ornaments from tunics and the weft-loop weaves used as small hangings with classical and Christian themes. The Christian custom of burying the deceased in the desert sands,

dressed in a tunic together with other textile items, has preserved these remarkable remnants of the past. (See plate 1, figures 68 and 69)

Silk weaving and sericulture have, according to Chinese legend, a history four thousand years old. The Han Dynasty (206 B.C.-220 A.D.) tomb of the Lady of Dai, a recent archeological discovery, yielded large quantities of silk robes, skirts, shoes, mittens, a banner, and even rolls of uncut silk in tabby, patterned weaves, and gauze.[16] Trade silks traveled the 'silk road' to the Roman Empire, and weaving with silk was done in the West during the Byzantine era. Some of these Byzantine silk brocades have been found in western church treasuries and even in Coptic graves.

Embroidery, silk tapestry—called k'o-ssu—and patterned weaves all reached a high level of sophistication in early China. The traditional art form continued through the different dynasties to leave a rich legacy of court costumes and palace hangings now in museum collections. (see plate 2, figures 53, 54, 55, and 66)

Far removed from the sophisticated textile technology of both the Orient and the Pre-Christian West, the ancient Peruvians developed highly diversified skills for working fibers into fabrics. Not only were they virtuoso weavers, but also skillful with basketry, net, lace, and embroidery techniques. Paracas, the name of a sand-blowing wind and of a west coast desert peninsula where domed caverns containing

elaborately clothed mummies have been discovered, refers to a cultural period of time circa 300 B.C.-200 A.C.[17] A mummy bundle from Paracas Peru might contain ponchos, turbans, tunics, mantles, skirts, dolls, and other fabric accoutrements along with jewelry and humble baskets of weaving implements. Natural cottons and alpaca were dyed with cochineal, indigo, and a wide range of other dyes to produce a broad and brilliant palette. The unbroken thread of that textile tradition can be followed from the Pre-Columbian period to the present. (see plates 3 and 4, figure 71)

There are also epic embroideries and monumental tapestries from the Medieval world, exquisite laces from Baroque and Victorian Europe, and ethnic fabrics unique in style and structure from more recent cultures. I find great personal inspiration in these ancient, antique, and anthropological fabrics. I feel an affinity for those artisans who worked with reverence for their craft. The two thousand year old fragments from Egypt and Peru retain a sense of immediacy that only happens when there is an intimate contact between the heart, hands, and handwork. Though the fabrications are as disparate as brocades and burial bundles, tapestries and tatting, rya rugs and royal robes, the essential connections— the stitches—have been universal throughout the web of civilization.

This chapter is an album of ideas inspired by art fabrics from other times and places. Possible ways of creating that are based on unusual combinations of constructional and accessory techniques are suggested and illustrated with examples from museums, from my own collection, from my own work and that of other artists and students.

Ideas from disparate cultures and crafts are synthesized, so there is no chronological order to "An Album of Ideas". Instead, there is a certain structural logic to the different sections.

Openwork tabbies, transparent tabbies, and gauze weaves designed for the contrast of opaque and translucent areas is first. The techniques, stitches, and fabrics are from China, Peru, antique openwork embroidery, and contemporary canvaswork.

Supplementary wefts that brocade, pattern, form weft-loops, or stitch on raised warps draw together Coptic weft-loop weaves, Colonial overshot weaves, Chinese couching, Moorman weaves, and contemporary weft-draping.

Weft-faced fabrics that are interlaced, twined, wrapped, looped, chained, and knotted bring together traditions from a pre-historic Oregon cave culture, a Pacific Northwest Coast Indian tribe, Ching Dynasty China, Coptic Egypt, Persia, and Peru.

Victorian and Paracas lace techniques, so distinctly different in materials, color, scale, and iconography are structurally similar and suggest unique ways of working with warp and stitching wefts.

Such diverse combinations require a sensitive approach to design. Integration—of materials, palette, and structure—is the prime concern. Repeating materials, colors, and the type of stitch within the structure and upon the structure will keep the stitching from seeming superfluous. Be sure that any stitch used is relevant to the design. Be selective.

The weaver can achieve this design integration with thoughtful planning, so that all is coordinated before construction begins. The stitchery artist can control integration with a careful selection of compatible fabrics and working threads. Threads can even be withdrawn from a cut edge of the fabric to use for stitching. The density of the weave, the nature of the materials, the harmonized colors, the stitches selected, and the way they are used should all compliment theme and design.

Only a few of the ideas suggested use a four-harness loom or complex draft. The cardboard loom, frame-loom or any simple two-harness system for tabby or tapestry would work. A stretched warp or fabric, needle, and stitching element are all that is needed in some instances.

Learn to see the warp as a stitching foundation where every connection of element to element contributes to the quality of the final fabrication.

Now, when all connections are vague
Often shoddy
More often adhesive than cohesive
It is imperative that designers understand . . .
The interrelationships of the whole to the parts.
Jack Lenor Larsen
"Time Was and Is"

1. Antique Openwork

There are openwork weaving techniques—gauze, Spanish Lace, Danish Medallion, and some loom-controlled lace weaves—and openwork embroidery techniques—deflected thread work, pulled thread, drawn thread, withdrawn element work, drawn fabric work, needleweaving, cut-fabric work and others. Translated from technique to structure—and forgetting names—the similarities are apparent. Penetrations in the surface of the fabric form negative spaces by grouping warp and weft elements with interlacing, wrapping, looping, chaining, or knotting as either a constructional or accessory technique. The lacunae, interstices, and interconnections become the design elements.

The weaver can design the fabric for this openwork by controlling the sett, spacing, drafting, and manual techniques. The non-weaver can select a fabric for its potential.

The stitches on the following chart will work across open warp areas. A row of stitches worked on grouped warp ends will create interesting negative spaces. Two rows of a stitch worked in opposite directions will create a countered pattern. Rows of a stitch or rows of different stitches might be used together in an open area. See the instructions (Methods 1, 2, and 3) in project 7 for ways to keep tabby wefts from sliding out of position into open warp areas.

There are so many ways to create openwork fabrics other than the traditional stitches—

gauze, Spanish Lace, Danish Medallion and Brook's Bouquet. Approach the problem of openwork with a new vocabulary of stitches and an open mind.

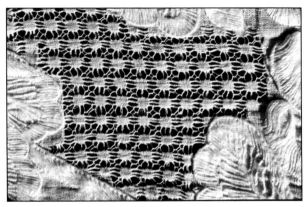
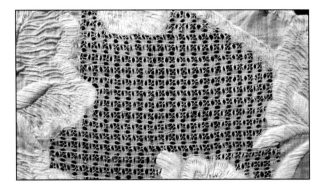

Figures 47, 48, and 49: Three details from an antique doily with both surface stitchery and openwork patterns. Warp or weft elements have been withdrawn from 3"×4" areas and then stitches used to pattern and embellish the remaining woven areas.

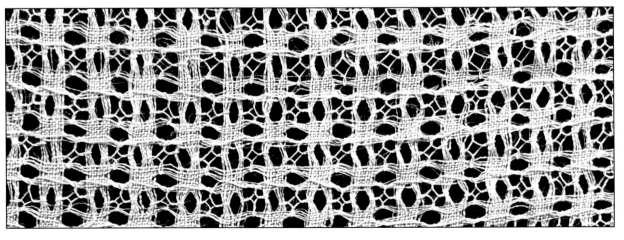

Part Two: An Album of Ideas   33

STITCHES FOR OPENWORK

I-10	W-1	L-1	C-1	K-1
I-14	W-7	L-5	C-4	K-4
I-16	W-9	L-8	C-11	K-6
I-17	W-13	L-9		K-13
I-21	W-15	L-13		K-14
I-22	W-18	L-17		K-15
I-23	W-20	L-20		K-16
	W-30	L-25		K-17
	W-33	L-28		K-24
	W-42	L-31		K-25
	W-45	L-32		K-33
	W-50	L-33		
	W-52	L-34		
	W-57	L-40		
	W-62	L-43		
	W-63	L-46		
		L-50		
		L-51		
		L-52		

Figure 50: Two rows of looping stitches worked on an open warp area. (L-1, L-5)

Figure 51: Two rows of a 'raised chain' stitch—a loop and wrap combination—work in opposite directions on groups of warp threads. (L-46)

Figure 52: Five rows of knotting stitches form a diamond network upon groups of warp threads. (K-1)

2. Chinese and Peruvian Gauze

The Chinese embroidered upon silk gauze two thousand years ago.[18] Members of the Manchu Court in eighteenth and nineteenth century China would wear multi-layers of shimmering gauze robes embroidered with gold and silk.[19] Long sleeve bands of k'o-ssu, gauze, or satin embroidered with silk were worn by the women of the court. Cut, color, and symbol designated rank in that highly stratified society.

A more recent Chinese textile in my collection is a natural silk gauze with a very fine warp and a multi-filament weft. The open meshes in the gauze are embroidered with stitches that draw pagodas, people, flowers, and trees in colorful silk threads. (I-23, W-62, W-63)

A Sicilian 'fishnet' embroidery tradition uses a natural linen gauze with colorful floral motifs and patterns in various stitches.[20]

Gauze, as a foundation fabric for designs, is also a Pre-Columbian Peruvian tradition.[21] A detail from a shirt panel in the Seattle Art Museum is shown in plate 4. The cotton and alpaca piece is attributed to the Chimu Culture (ca. 1000-1470 A.D.) Tapestry, gauze, and coiled roundels with tassels combine in a lively sculptural surface of open penetrations, flat figural areas, and high textural relief. Intensely rhythmic, the piece speaks of ceremonial dance. (I-6, I-23, W-23)

China, Europe, or Peru—whatever the inspiration—gauze can be a foundation fabric for designs in tapestry and embroidery.

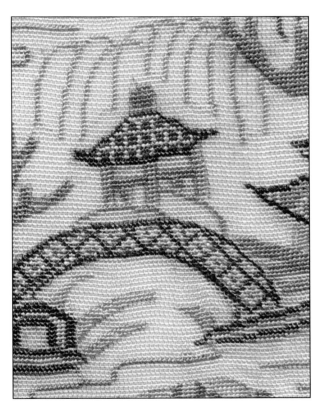

Figure 53: A detail from the embroidered panel.

Figure 54: Pavilions, bridges, willow trees, bamboo, and floral motifs are stitched in colorful silk threads on the gauze weave fabric.

3. Transparent Weaves

Translucent light filtering fabrics with richly textured opaque areas can be created in different ways. The fabric is essentially the same, an openweave tabby or other threading, but the method of filling in the opaque areas differs.

Needlepoint or canvaswork is an accessory technique. The textile is an openmesh weave, the stitches are mostly wrapping stitches and are selected to cover the fabric completely. If the ground cloth is handsome and the stitching elements complementary to warp and weft, the accessory stitches need not cover the entire piece. The design could play on the contrast of solid and open areas. If the finishing is fine, the piece could be viewed from obverse or reverse sides. (W-17)

A detail of an embroidered goldfish on gauze from a late 19th century silk Chinese Sleeveband. Murray Warner Collection of Oriental Art, Jordan Schnitzer Museum of Art, University of Oregon, MWCH44:33.

4. Brocading

B rocading would be another method for contrasting opaque and transparent areas in a design. Brocading wefts that are supplementary to the main weft can be inlaid or overlaid. A transparent tabby weave with inlaid supplementary wefts can use either the positive or negative areas as the prominent part of the design. The relationship between warp, weft, and brocading weft must be perfectly balanced so that the inlaid element does not distort the rows of tabby. The supplementary wefts, instead of being interlaced, could be worked with other

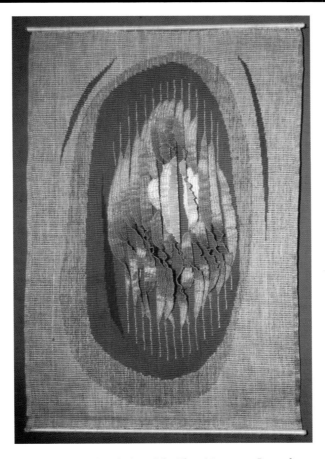

"Encrusted Gold and Flame" by Theo Moorman. Brocading is combined with a series of draped bands in a weaving that makes an interesting departure from the rigid rectangle dictated by the nature of weaving. Photo courtesy of the Moorman Trust.

stitches to add interest to the figure or motif. The warp areas reserved for the design field or background could also be worked with a variety of stitches to bind warp and weft.

Brocading wefts that overlay the ground weave can be used with plain weaves, twill, or another threading such as the Moorman weave. (Shuttle Spindle and Dyepot, Winter '81) The fabric for overlaid brocading may be either transparent or opaque, and the enriched areas need not be limited to interlacing. Stitches that wrap, loop, chain, and knot or create weft-loops or weft-pile can be worked on the warp.

5. Stitching on Raised Warps

If the tie-up of the loom is planned for a single harness lift there is an interesting stitching option available: the single harness can be raised and that set of warp elements used as the foundation for stitches. (fig. 45) By weaving picks of the ground weave, then stitching upon the raised warps, the stitches are spaced as floats are spaced, and they tend to overlay the ground weave. The texture and character of the stitches becomes more prominent. Remember, any stitch that works upon warp will work on these raised warp sets, but with quite a different effect than stitching on the ground warp. See the openwork chart for stitch suggestions.

You can create the same effect on any other loom system by simply skipping warps in a regular or irregular order, weaving one or two picks and then stitching again on a select set of warps.

A pattern threading and treadling could be followed with stitches worked between the tabby rows as in an overshot weave. Imagine a rosepath with wrapping stitches worked on the pattern harnesses. The same diamonds or diagonals would appear, but with the clarity of a more prominent supplementary element.

Figure 57: A detail from a tussah silk sampler showing both brocading and stitches worked on raised warp threads. A Moorman threading system was used.

Many drafts create distinct motifs—diamond shaped, round, or floral—that can be used in combination with tabby areas. These patterns

Figure 58: "Bicentennial Caftan" by Nancy Arthur Hoskins.

Figure 59: A detail of the scalloped border worked with the needle and with the shuttle.

Figure 60: A detail of the reverse side of the same border showing how the pattern wefts float across on the back of the fabric.

end abruptly when the treadling changes to tabby. By analyzing the patterns and then selectively interlacing certain areas with a needle you can achieve a more graceful finish to the pattern. The scalloped finish on the border of the dress (fig. 58) was worked this way to eliminate the new pattern beginning in the interval between the petals. The tabby wefts were carried in the shuttle, but the pattern wefts worked in with the needle going under the warp and out again to keep the petals intact. (fig. 59-60)

A draft can be planned especially for warp or weft floats and those floats used as the foundation for other stitches. Penelope Drooker's warp float sampler is illustrated in fig. 61.

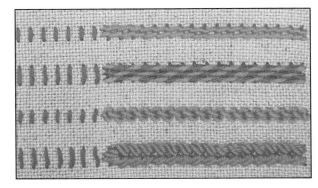

A sampler of stitches on warp floats by Penelope Drooker author of Embroidering with the Loom. *Photo credit: P. Drooker.*

7. Coptic Weft-looping

Coptic weavers used weft-looping in combination with balanced plain weaves and with tapestry. (I-13) (See fig. 62 and plate 1)

The weft-loops might be of linen or colored wool and used to frame tapestry squares with a high relief area, or used to paint textured por-

traits and figures. The pieces that I have examined in the Stanford University Museum of Art and at the Metropolitan Museum of Art are done with a double or triple weft of wool or linen with the weft-loops sometimes frayed apart, but not cut. There are usually an uneven number of rows of tabby between the supplementary wefts so that they are tied down with opposite tabby picks. The technique is best described as a brocading weft with loops. Colors are juxtaposed or subtly shaded to suggest pattern and painting with the discontinuous supplementary wefts.

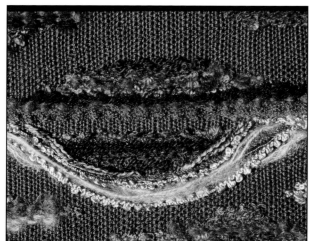

Figure 62: A Coptic textile from the Iris & B. Gerald Cantor Center for the Visual Arts at Stanford University was a gift from Timothy Hopkins. The square panel with amphorae, animals, and plants has a wool and linen tapestry area surrounded by linen weft-loops.

Figure 63: "Caldera" detail by Nancy Arthur Hoskins. The multi-strand swags span several picks before being tied down. 15"×25"

Macro-loops fashioned with brocading wefts, as an expansion of this concept, can be used with a tabby, pattern, or Moorman threading. I have used this technique in different ways. "Caldera", on a Moorman threading, has multi-strand swags that span wide spaces and several picks before being tied down. (fig. 63) The brocading wefts in "When the Vine Maple Turns", (plate 12) a Moorman draft, and "Macro-maple Leaf", (fig. 64) an overshot draft, drape across a one foot space between the panels. "Gift of the Sea", (fig. 65) on tabby and turned 90 degrees, is designed around the rhythm of the draped brocading wefts that are carried across two or three inches of weaving.

"Denouement" (plate 10-11) is a three paneled tapestry that hangs on a stair wall in the entry of the Lane Community College Performing Arts Theater. The three panels symbolize the three acts of a drama, and the multi-colored brocading wefts the entwined lives of the characters. The brocading technique plays structurally on the meaning of the theatrical term 'denouement'— to untie or to undo the knots in the plot. The brocading wefts are knotted upon the tie-down warps in the central panel and knotted upon themselves in the drapes, but merely set in the raised shed in the first and last panel. (K-1)

Weft-loops, swags, and drapes with brocading threads, inspired by the weaving of the Copts can be translated into the contemporary idiom.

Figure 64: "Macro-maple Leaf" by Nancy Arthur Hoskins. 5'×11' The pattern wefts drape across a one foot span between the two panels. Commissioned by Dr. and Mrs. William Parshall.

Figure 65: "Gift of the Sea" by Nancy Arthur Hoskins. 5'×3'. The brocading wefts are carried across several inches of weaving before being tied down. Commissioned by Dr. and Mrs. Louis Marzano.

8. Couching

A 'couched' thread is one that is laid upon a fabric and then attached with other stitches. Precious metallic threads or threads that will not go in and out of a fabric with ease are attached this way. Many accessory stitches can be used for couching down or stitching down an element. Couched threads in accessory work can be compared to supplementary pattern or brocading wefts in weaving, to supplementary elements carried within rows of stitches to strengthen nets and laces, or to rigid elements encased within rows of stitches in baskets. The couched element is passive, almost like a passenger, and is supplementary to the binding system.

Supplementary elements could just as well be attached to warp or woven fabrics for interesting surface effects. A knotting stitch (K-1, K-2) with a very fine weight sewing thread or invisible thread could make the stitching element disappear. Curvilinear designs, often hard to achieve in the rectilinear woven structure, could be emphasized with couched elements. The

Figure 66: A detail from a Chinese purse cover. The gold background threads are couched to the fabric. The vase with flowers is done with colored silk threads in a Chinese knot stitch outlined with wrapped threads. (K-20, W-9)

couching element, free of any structural responsibility, can be freely manipulated between the tie-down stitiches.

Objects as well as extra elements can be couched or attached to the surface with a variety of ways. The lace stitches that will work around and around can sculpt small cups that will contain pebbles, shells, or beads. Feathers can be wrapped at the base of the quill and stitched to warp or woven areas. You are only limited to maintaining the integrity of the design concept.

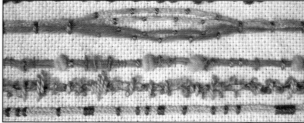

Figure 67: A detail from a sampler showing couched threads.

9. *Coptic, K'o-ssu, and Peruvian Tapestry*

A tapestry could be designed to explore the way that supplementary wrapping wefts were used in Coptic tapestries to outline, draw, and pattern. (W-58, W-59, W-60, W-61) Most often these were used in monochromatic weavings: the natural wool or linen as the color for the field and for the sketching weft, the darker dyed wool for the figure or motif. (fig. 68

Figure 68: A detail of a rabbit from a linen and wool Coptic tapestry fragment shows how the linen threads are used to draw details on the leaves and animal. Circa 500 A.D.

Figure 69: A detail of a lion and tree from a narrow Coptic tapestry band. The linen and wool areas are joined in a very regular pattern. The sides of the dark circles are formed with wefts that step and float. (W-60) Circa 500 A.D.

Figure 70: A k'o-ssu tapestry panel in silk and gold. The 'li shui', a rainbow of stripes representing upright water, is outlined with a gold weft that wraps, steps, and floats between the different color areas. (W-60) Late 19th or early 20th century.

and 69) The design might be representational or abstract, the wrapping wefts random or controlled in patterns.

'K'o-ssu" is the Chinese term for silk tapestry. Gold threads are used to outline color areas in a small fragment of k'o-ssu in my collection. The gold thread wraps around a warp, floats up several picks, and then wraps again very much as it does in some Coptic tapestries. (W-59) (plate 2, fig. 70) Structurally the pieces are very similar, yet the materials and motifs are so distinctly East and West.

Warp-wise wrapping on a single end can be observed in both Coptic and Peruvian tapestries, the technique used to define and draw details. (W-9) Warp-wise wrapping with the stitch alternating between a pair of warps is used for detailing, as well as small pattern units. (W-30) The intermixture of interlacing and wrapping imparts a rhythmic style to these tapestries so far apart in origin.

Figure 71: A small latticed alpaca tapestry with a costumed figure from Peru. Date unknown.

Looping, chaining, and knotting stitches, along with many variation and combination stitches, can create weft-faced fabrics. Each stitch will create a different surface texture and can be worked in continuous rows or alternated with rows of interlacing. Color changes can be made, just as they can be made in tapestry techniques. Because many of the stitches can construct in ways that move away from the warp plane— warp-wise lace edges or lace overlays—they can form a very plastic surface. Open areas with eccentric shapes can be reserved with rows of knotting stitches as a contrast to solid weft areas. The open warps are then used as a foundation for decorative stitches.

Photo credit: Alexis Garrett.

Figure 72: "Oregon Spring" by Nancy Arthur Hoskins. The quilted and padded tapestry has a central panel worked with the needle and an applied fringe. (W-30, W-39)

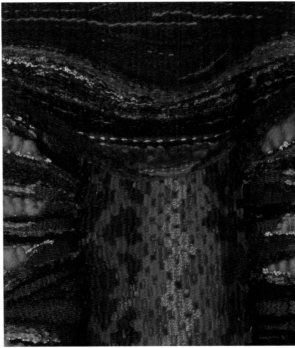

Photo credit: Alexis Garrett.

Figure 73: Detail from "Oregon Spring" showing the padded tapestry areas and needlelace band.

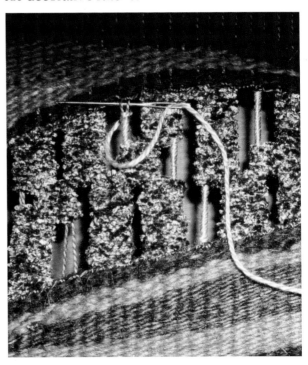

Figure 74 : A detail from the author's tapestry "Open Spaces" showing wrapping stitches on single or pairs of warp ends. (W 9, W-30)

The following chart lists stitches that could be combined with tapestry or weft-faced plain weave structures.

☐ *DIAGRAMS*

STITCHES FOR WEFT-FACE AREAS

Stitches for solidly filled weft areas

I-6	W-1	L-1	C-1	K-1
I-11	W-4	L-5	C-4	K-4
I-12	W-6	L-31	C-11	K-6
I-13	W-7	L-32		K-24
I-15	W-15	L-46		K-33
I-18	W-18			
I-19	W-19			
I-20	W-33			
I-21	W-35			
	W-42			
	W-45			
	W-50			
	W-57			
	W-58			
	W-59			
	W-60			
	W-61			

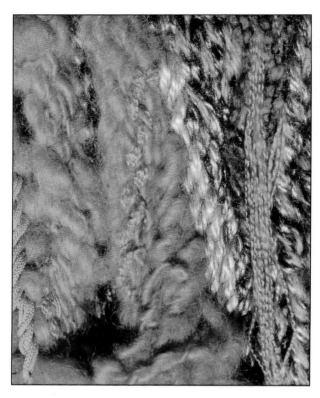

Figure 75: A detail from "Lichen" showing a wide band of needlelace (L-13)

STITCHES FOR WEFT-FACE AREAS

Warp-wise stitches

W-9	L-8	K-13
W-12	L-9	
W-13	L-13	
W-20	L-17	
W-30	L-20	
	L-23	
	L-25	
	L-28	
	L-33	
	L-34	
	L-40	
	L-50	
	L-51	
	L-52	

Stitches to hold open warp areas

I-14	C-1	K-1
	C-4	K-4
		K-6

11. *The Bakhtiyari Bedding Bag*

I have a nineteenth century Southern Persian weaving, once a bedding bag of the nomadic Bakhtiyari tribe.[22] The piece combines several techniques in an asymmetrical composition— weft-wrapping weave, weft-pile weave, weft-faced plain weave, and a brocaded tapestry area. The bag is sampler-like in its style. I sense that the mother did the visible side of the bag, and that a daughter was allowed to experiment with geese and stripes, tapestry and brocading on the back: a very pragmatic and thrifty way to learn. The design is totally integrated with warm vegetable dyed colors, and made ever interesting with the textural and pattern changes. The weaving speaks of an ancient and proud tradition being passed on to a new generation.

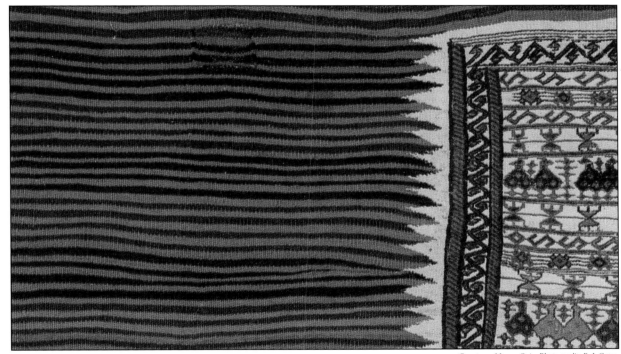

Courtesy of James Opie. Photo credit: P. J. Gates.

Figure 76: A late 19th century Bakhtiyari bedding bag from Southern Persia. 3'11"×5", wool warp and weft.

Figure 77: The tapestry woven stripes.

Courtesy of James Opie. Photo credit: P. J. Gates.

Figure 78: The brocaded tapestry area with geese and pattern motifs.

Figure 79: The weft-pile area.

Figure 80: The 'Soumak' or wrapped panel.

12. Chilkat Twining

The Chilkat blanket of the Pacific Northwest Coast Indians is a weft-faced twined fabric worked upon a warp-weighted loom. The designs are rich with totemic symbols and interesting structural details. The Chilkat weavers used two methods of twining. (I-14, W-57) Only a close examination of the structure can detect the different binding systems.

Working with the help of the loom—treadling, setting a weft in the shed, then stitching the second weft with the needle—expedites the twining process.

Twining is an ancient binding system. Twined artifacts from Catul Huyuk (in modern day Turkey) are dated 6000 B.C.[23] Twined mats and sandals from Fort Rock Cave in central Oregon, discovered by Dr. Luther Cresman of the University of Oregon, are even older and have a radio-carbon date of 7000 B.C. Over sixty sagebrush sandals, along with other basketry fragments, were found at pre-historic Fort Rock Cave.[24]

Figure 81: A Chilkat weft-faced textile in yellow, blue-green, white and black is of mountain goat hair with a warp fringe of goat hair and cedar bark. Photo courtesy of the University of Oregon Museum of Natural and Cultural History.

Figure 82: A pair of 9,000-year-old sagebrush sandals discovered in Oregon's Fort Rock cave by Dr. Luther Cressman, Professor Emeritus of the University of Oregon. Photo courtesy of the University of Oregon Museum of Natural and Cultural History. Photo credit: David Stone.

13. Doubleweave

The top layer of warp in a double weave could be used as the foundation for stitches with the bottom layer adding background color. (fig. 83) Stuffed double weave pockets or tubes could be quilted with stitches.

Figure 83: A detail of a row of gauze worked over a weft-faced doubleweave area from a loom sampler by Helen Brent, a Lane Community College weaving student.

14. Quilting

Quilting, a method of stitching layers of padding and fabric together, can be combined with tapestry or doubleweave. High relief tapestry can be made by stuffing and then quilting to a firm background fabric. Eccentric weft areas in tapestry have a natural tendency to bulge. You can design and weave to take advantage of this factor and plan for a sculptural stuffed and quilted fabrication. (See fig. 72-73)

The usual quilting stitch is an interlacing stitch. (I-2) One that I prefer is the wrapping stitch (W-15), but spaced somewhat so that on the surface it resembles an interlacing stitch.

15. *Victorian Needlelace*

Years ago, in a dusty old trunk, I found a piece of unfinished needlework. The lace tapes were still stitched to the fabric foundation, the needle stuck into the fabric, and the ball of linen thread waiting. I was puzzled by the tiny stitches seemingly done in the air. They were obviously familiar stitches, but worked upon threads, not fabric. 'Needlelace' has fascinated me ever since the discovery of that bit of Victorian lace.

Needlelace is done in two ways. Bobbin or machine-made lace tapes are basted to a fabric foundation following a pattern. The stitches begin on the tape edges and then construct lace in the open areas. Another method begins with long stitches sewn in a pattern upon a fabric or paper, and those stitches used as the foundation elements for the lace. Diminutive stitches make this the most dainty of all lacework. Needlelace, more than any other craft, bridges the gap between constructional and accessory stitching because it is both. (fig. 84-85)

Tapes could be constructed as a bobbin lace technique, or of something unusual like inkle weaving or tablet weaving. The colors and materials of the tape to be repeated in the lace stitches.

An idea is borrowed from Pre-Columbian Peru for weaving a latticed textile by spacing and grouping the warp and weft: the plain weave either balanced or weft-faced, the open squares or rectangles to be filled with those needlelace stitches that span spaces. (See fig. 71) The piece could be worked as a sampler or with motifs or figures stitched in the open spaces. The tapestry or tabby areas could be used for further development of the design.

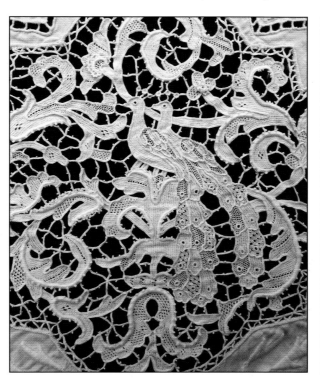

Figure 84: Needlelace peacocks from a tablecloth that combines needlelace with cut-fabric work, surface stitchery, and filet lace in floral and figural motifs. courtesy of Jean Cook of Olympia, Washington.

Figure 85: A detail of a needlelace doily with bobbin lace tapes forming the floral pattern.

16. Antique Filet Lace

A knotted meshwork fabric called 'filet lace' can be constructed with the technique used to make fishing nets or with a needle technique. It could also be simulated upon the loom. The warp sett should be slightly less dense than that for a balanced weave so that a knotting stitch can be used to create square, triangular, or diamond shaped meshes. (K-14, K-15, K-16, K-17)

Traditional filet lace is a white-on-white fabric with motifs, patterns, and pictures stitched upon the square meshes. Interlacing is the most common stitch used and the small squares completely filled in with bits of plain weave done with a needle, but many other stitches can also be used.

Peruvian net fabrics were worked with a knot at the binding point of two warps and two wefts.[25] Birds, fish, and little figures were stitched as outlines, solid tapestry filled shapes, spot or overall patterns. The impractical fabrics seem too delicate to have survived for over a thousand years.

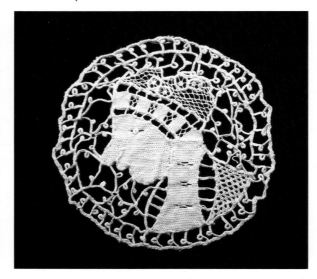

Figure 86: A filet lace butterfly and three needlelace butterflies from Belgium. The filet lace courtesy of Lea Cook of Roseburg, Oregon.

Figure 87: A needlelace portrait worked by the grandmother of Kathryn Weaver of Olympia, Washington.

Figure 88: A filet lace portrait from the lace tablecloth. Courtesy of Jean Cook of Olympia, Washington.

17. *Peruvian Weaving and Needlework*

There is a rare and wonderful fabric from Paracas Culture Peru (ca. 300 B.C.-200 A.D.) in the Brooklyn Museum. Both the ground weave and border are unusual in construction. (fig. 89-90) The mask motifs in the central panel are of warps wrapped with colored threads that are then interlaced with the weft. (W-13)[26] The way that the masks appear within the structure of the weave seems magical and mythical. As in ancient Peru, plan a plain weave warp that is not too closely sett and use warps wrapped with colored threads for the design. (W-13, I-1, K-4)

The border of this Paracas piece is a frieze of over ninety Lilliputian three-dimensional figures. Each figure is worked with a wrapping stitch (W-21) going around and around to form a tiny tubular fabric.[27] There is another ceremonial mantle in the Goteborg Etnografiska Museum in Sweden that is constructed entirely of this stitch. (Interweave, Fall '80) A circlet of birds and flowers from the Seattle Art Museum is also made with this technique, which resembles knitting. (plate 3) The stitch can be started upon a single element, warp, fabric, or stitches upon

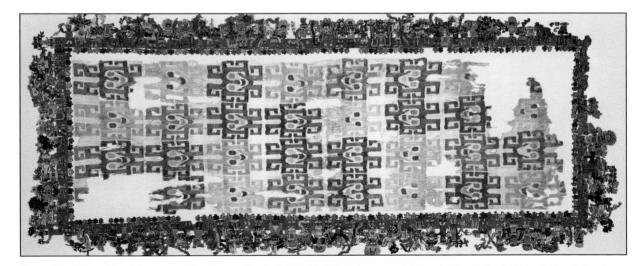

Figure 89: A Nasca Mantle known as "The Paracas Textile." 100-300 C.E. Cotton, camelid fiber, textile: 58 ¼ x 24 ½ in. (148 x 62.2 cm). Brooklyn Museum, John Thomas Underwood Memorial Fund, 38.121. Photo courtesy of the Brooklyn Museum.

Figure 90: Details from the frieze of figures on the upper left hand corner and three figures from the lower right hand border of the Paracas mantle. (W-18) Photo courtesy of the Brooklyn Museum.

fabric and can be combined with weaving in many interesting ways.

Looping stitches and knotted looping stitches were used in this same way to sculpt small figures upon clothing and other Peruvian pieces. The stitches were dense and the yarns very fine. (L-13, L-34, L-52)

The Nazca Culture of Peru closely parallels the time span for the Paracas Culture. Nazca needlework examples, primarily in the accessory wrapping stitch, are of flying figures, felines, and mythological creatures stitched onto plain weave backgrounds.

Harriet Tidball suggests in *Peru: Textiles Unlimited* that, "rich and harmonious combinations of stitchery with textiles of special structures and color-designs and area planning," are an unexplored territory for handweavers of our time. The Peruvian techniques, more than those of any other culture, are a constant source of wonder and admiration for the contemporary craftsman—a catalyst to creativity.

Figure 91: A small sample of a tubular tulip worked in the same technique as the figures in the Goteborg and Brooklyn Museum's Paracas Mantles. (W-18)

18. *Weaving Fabric for Stitchery*

I learned to weave so that I could design and create my own background fabric for stitchery, but the interest in using stitches as a part of the constructional process has taken precedence over that initial goal. Only once have I woven fabric specifically for an embroidery. (fig. 92) That tabby fabric of tussah silk and rayon uses a draped warp section as a part of the design. Accessory stitches layer row upon row in a pastel rainbow and emphasize the warp drape with a small chained band that floats between the panels.

"Willamette Winter", a small soft sculpture, began with a gold-flecked place mat of Willamette Valley linen woven by Ruth B. Wheeler. Many stitchery techniques are combined in the piece—reverse applique with layers of velour, shisha mirror embroidery, accessory stitching, needlelace bands, quilting, gathering, and stuffing. Spider webs, knots, wrapped knots, and looping stitches work upon the linen fabric. The white-on-white color scheme is enhanced by the high relief, the subtle glitter of the gold weft, and the reflections in the mirrors. (fig. 94)

I have been creating a series of miniature silk tapestries worked on one long warp. Each new section of warp is approached as if it were a

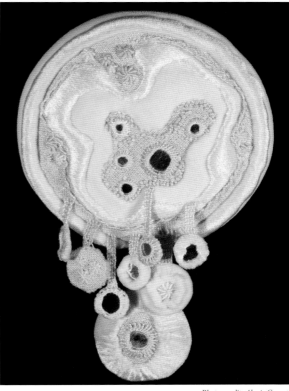

Photo credit: Alexis Garrett.

Figure 94: "Willamette Winter" by Nancy Arthur Hoskins. A soft sculpture combining reverse applique, surface stitching, quilting, padding, shisha mirror embroidery, and needlelace. Willamette Valley linen and velour with cotton and silk stitching elements. 10"×10", 1974.

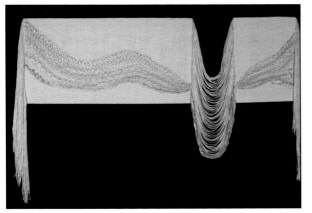

Photo credit: Alexis Garrett.

Figure 92: "Somewhere" by Nancy Arthur Hoskins, tabby weave, tussah silk and rayon warp and weft, silk, wool, and cotton stitching elements. 4'×1-1/2'. 1979.

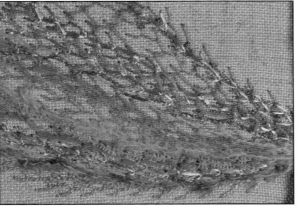

Photo credit: Alexis Garrett.

Figure 93: A detail from "Somewhere" showing the layered looping stitches. (L-21)

blank canvas. Each encounter of warp and weft becomes an option for a design choice. The shuttle, butterfly, and needle are used interchangeably to achieve the desired effect. The tapestries are an attempt to express that intimate and precious quality that I have observed in the ancient Egyptian, Chinese, and Peruvian art fabrics.

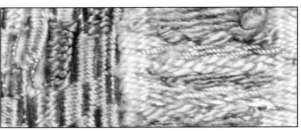

Figure 96: Detail from "Today" (W-30)

Figure 95: "Today" by Nancy Arthur Hoskins, 6"×9", cotton warp, silk and gold wefts and stitching elements. 1981.

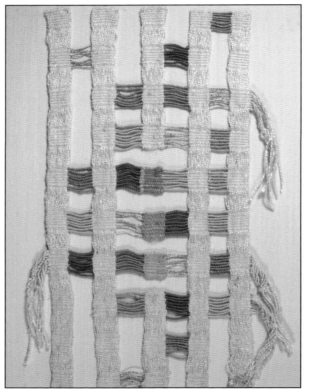

Figure 97: "Dawn" by Nancy Arthur Hoskins, 6"×9", cotton warp, silk and gold wefts and stitching elements. 1981.

I would hope that those of you who stitch, but do not weave might be inspired to do so by the projects and ideas suggested in this book. You will discover that all of the skills mastered with embroidery and other needle techniques will be valuable in learning to weave. Tapestry, especially, is compatible with a needlework background. I hope that weavers have discovered new ways of using stitches. This method of learning a small vocabulary of stitches, before beginning loom weaving, is based on the philosophy that one learns the basic connections and then how they are used to achieve different functional and artistic purposes.

Somehow it doesn't seem fair to teach skills that will require even more time and patience than what you are already doing—weaving and embroidering. The needle cannot compete with the shuttle for speed, but it can bring a calligraphic quality to woven work. There are new challenges for those of you interested in aesthetics, and sensitive to the logic of structure as a basis for learning the fiber arts.

Figure 98: Detail from "Dawn". (W-10)

I no longer draw clear demarcations between weaving, embroidery, and other fiber crafts, but tend to view all through the magnifying glass as one-on-one stitches. The character of that initial connection influences structure, process, and design, and distinguishes the skill of the artisan. Too often, the habit of history, the mechanization of the method, and the diversity of the final fabrication obscures the importance of that "essential connection". Artificial barriers between the crafts have developed over the centuries.

Time was and is
when a craftsman knew fabric as fleece . . .
Jack Lenor Larsen
"Time Was and Is"

The fiber arts are universal and intertwined with the history of civilization. Fabric fragments thousands of years old from far corners of the earth are poignant reminders of man's basic need for clothing, containers, and ceremony.

Bone needles predate even the earliest of textile finds. The Bible speaks of,

"a hanging . . . of blue, and purple, and scarlet, and fine twined linen with needlework."
Exodus 36:37

Weaving and embroidery are ancient traditions, but there are always new ways of working with old techniques—infinite possibilities. An idea must, however, filter through your imagination and the magic of your fingers to become a fabrication. Inspiration without skill is an empty wish, and so, the final section of the book is to help you develop your stitching skills.

Photo credit: Alexis Garrett.

Figure 99: "Between the Clouds" by Nancy Arthur Hoskins, 6"×9", cotton warp, silk and gold wefts and stitching elements. 1981.

Photo credit: Alexis Garrett.

Figure 100: Detail from "Between the Clouds". (L-8)

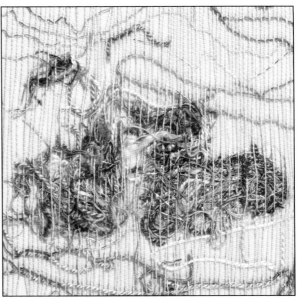

Photo credit: Alexis Garrett.

Figure 101: Detail from "Bits and Pieces of Today."

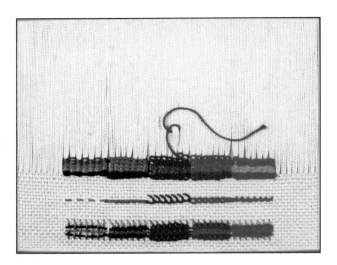

Five Stitches for:
Photo credit: Alexis Garrett.

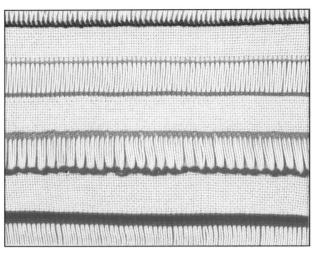

Hems
Photo credit: Alexis Garrett.

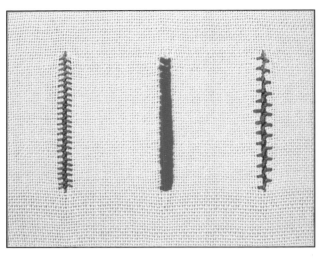

Joins
Photo credit: Alexis Garrett.

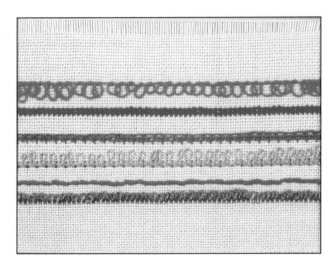

Textures
Photo credit: Alexis Garrett.

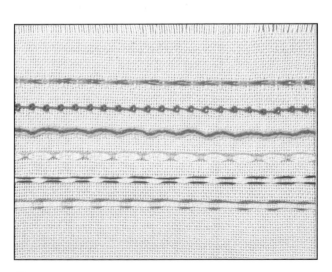

Floats
Photo credit: Alexis Garrett.

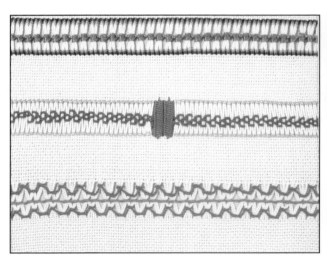

Openwork
Photo credit: Alexis Garrett.

58

PART THREE: The Stitches

Step-by-step directions and diagrams for the five basic stitches, plus one hundred and ninety-five of their variations and combinations are contained in this last section of the book. I hope that the consistency of the directions and diagrams will contribute to their clarity and your ease of learning. The section is designed to work as a visual index of stitches. The five stitches and stitch families are arranged in their structural order: interlacing, wrapping, looping, chaining, and knotting.

This order was organized to collate certain constructional and accessory stitches for teaching purposes. Not all stitches, or stitch families are included, and this order represents a personal opinion. This method of organization first took form for a slide lecture presented at Convergence '78 and was then written in thesis form as a final project for my Master's Degree in Fine Arts: Weaving, Art Education, and Art History at the University of Oregon in that same year. It has subsequently served as a teaching method for guild and conference workshops and for university classes.

□ THE STITCHES
The five stitches are arranged on a continuum that describes their increasing complexity.

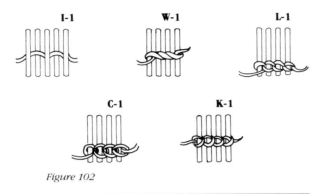

I-1   W-1   L-1

C-1   K-1

Figure 102

□ THE STITCH FAMILIES
All stitches within each family are structurally similar, their way of working as a binding unit in constructional crafts comparable to the way they work as an accessory stitch upon fabric.

Figure 103

The stitches in each family follow a general order—
First the basic stitch—

W-1

Figure 104

Then, variations upon different foundations—

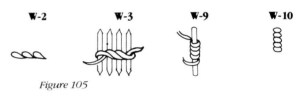

W-2   W-3   W-9   W-10

Figure 105

Then related or identical stitches that work in different directions—

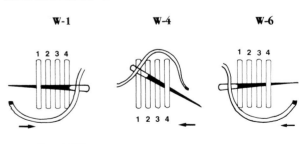

W-1   W-4   W-6

1 2 3 4   1 2 3 4

1 2 3 4

Figure 106

Or stitches that work upon different faces of the foundation—

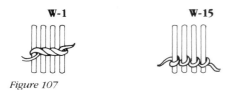

Figure 107

Next are combinations which can be—
Two stitches done as one—

Figure 108

A pair of stitches used together—

Figure 109

Stitches worked with two elements—

W-57

Figure 110

Or a row of stitches upon a row of stitches—

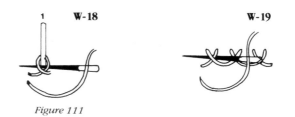

Figure 111

□ *THE DIRECTION AND DIAGRAM PAGES*
Each instructional page follows this format—

Numbers:
Stitches are initialed by the first letter of the family name—

I . . . . .Interlacing Stitches
W . . . . .Wrapping Stitches
L . . . . .Looping Stitches
C . . . . .Chaining Stitches
K . . . . .Knotting Stitches
And numbered sequentially within each family—

I-1
I-2
I-3

The identification number is cited in the left column and at the far right within the box that illustrates the finished stitch.

W-3

Figure 113

No.	Foundation	Names	Directions	Diagrams	Stitch
I-1	warp	**interlacing stitch** weaving darning stitch cloth stitch	Work weft-wise from right to left. 1. The needle goes under warp 5, over warp 4, under warp 3, over warp 2, under warp 1.	1 2 3 4 5 1. 2.	I-1
I-2	fabric	**interlacing stitch** running stitch	Work weft-wise from right to left. 1. Come out at a. Go in at b — out at c — in at d — out at e — in at f — out at g.	g f e d c b a 1. 2.	I-2

Figure 112

Foundation:

The stitching foundations are cited in the second column. Certain stitches work in exactly the same way on a variety of foundations. The first set of three diagrams for each family illustrates how the same stitch works upon warp, fabric, and upon stitches worked upon fabric. Because a stitch worked on a set of warp elements and a stitch worked on a set of stitches on fabric is done essentially the same way, the accessory version is not repeated for other stitches. Instead, that foundation 'stitches on fabric' will be the indication that the stitch will work that way. There are many stitches other than the basic five that work both ways.

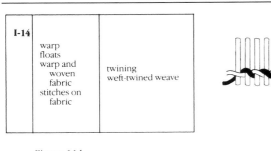

Figure 114

The foundation for stitching may be only a single element. Single element foundations are diagrammed in different ways depending upon how the stitch is working. The single element might be—

a single warp   a weft-wise element   a ring

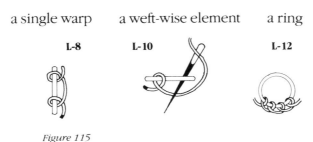

L-8   L-10   L-12

Figure 115

or a single element working continuously upon itself

C-7

Figure 116

Whether the single element foundation is warp-wise, weft-wise, spiralling, diagonal,

Figure 117: Diminutive spider webs from a piece of European needlelace. Courtesy of Nancy Hughes of Eugene, Oregon.

ringed, or working continuously upon itself the one-on-one relationship is the same. The stitching element works upon only a portion of the single element. If it's a hawser tied to a bollard or a minute filet lace knot, it is structurally identical.

Figure 118: A pine needle basket bottom decorated with a spider web and other stitches. Courtesy of Ellen Dorothea Lindsay, my mother, of Morro Bay, California.

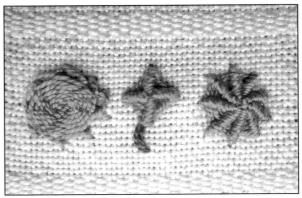

Figure 119: Spider webs from a loom woven sampler.

The foundation may be a set of elements—

a pair a warp radiating elements

L-20 **L-5** **L-56**

Figure 120

The foundation may be a row of stitches—

L-13

Figure 121

The foundation may be warp and fabric—

L-55

Figure 122

The foundation may be—

fabric a fabric edge fabric edges

L-15 **L-16** **L-22**

Figure 123

stitches upon fabric

L-3

rows of stitches upon fabric

L-11

Figure 124

radiating stitches upon fabric

L-56

Figure 125

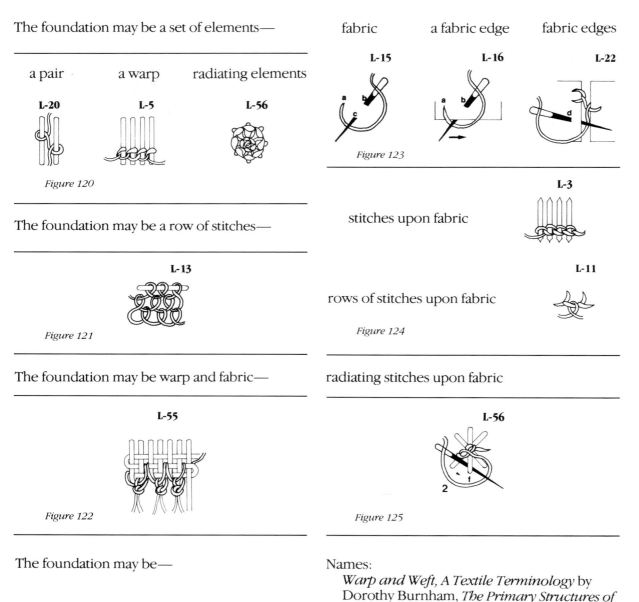

Names:
Warp and Weft, A Textile Terminology by Dorothy Burnham, *The Primary Structures of Fabrics* by Irene Emery, and *The Stitches of Creative Embroidery* by Jacqueline Enthoven were the texts used as references on stitch names and terminology.

Stitch names are listed in the third column. Stitch names, when dealing with both weaving and embroidery, are so confusing and redundant that they have been a major problem in organizing this information. Reference to a stitch is, therefore, usually made by number rather than name. If a name is in bold letters it indicates the name I have designated in this book for a basic stitch. I have taken that liberty with only the basic five stitches to emphasize structural similarities, and there was precedent for each name selected. Common names are listed by their association with a stitch and do not indicate any preference for the name. Traditional stitch family names in common usage are cited, even though a stitch may be included in a different structural group. When a name was at all questionable it was omitted. A 'looping stitch' is differentiated from the word 'loop' as it is used to describe a curved portion of an element.

There are universal stitches, but not universal names. Universal stitch names that relate to structure need to be decided upon by the authorities in the field, but that is in the future. Nomenclature is a complex and challenging problem that must be confronted so those in the fiber arts can cross communicate. We need,
"to raise new questions, new possibilities, to regard old problems from a new angle."
Albert Einstein and L. Infeld

Directions:

The directions begin with an indication of which way the row of stitches will go—

warp-wise   weft-wise

L-9   **L-10**

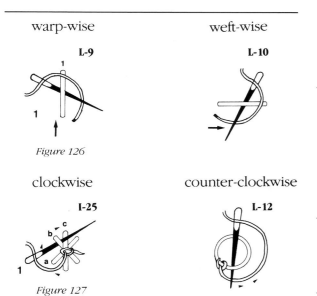

Figure 126

clockwise   counter-clockwise

I-25   **L-12**

Figure 127

The instruction numbers 1, 2, 3, relate to the diagrams showing the different steps. When two motions are done as one it is written this way—

1. Come out at a. Go in at b—out at c.

W-2

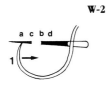

Figure 128

Diagrams:

Most diagrams are drawn from a working position at the loom, not always the easiest way to work a stitch. If you are not at the loom you can change to a more comfortable angle. Arrows indicate the direction of the row of stitches, not necessarily the direction of the needle.

W-1   **W-2**

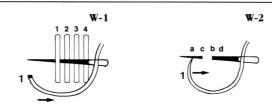

Figure 129

The end of the stitching element that is attached to the warp at the beginning is marked—

W-1

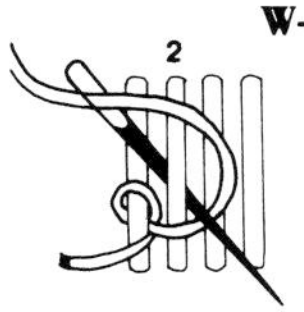

Figure 130

Warp elements are numbered to relate to loom threading—

I-9

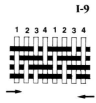

Figure 131

Small letters indicate where the needle goes in and out of the fabric—

L-14

Figure 132

Capital letters are used to represent a stitch upon fabric—

L-3

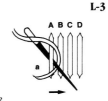

Figure 133

Illustrations of finished stitches are found in the last column along with the identification letter and number—

L-3

Figure 134

All stitches are drawn in a very regular, didactic way.
Only translation into fiber will make them exciting.
General stitching instructions can be found in "Part
One: The Learning Projects."

The author's silk tapestry "Reflections" inspired by Monet. Photo credit: Zachary Blaine Hoskins.

*The tapestry "Reflections" of fine silk thread is growing on the loom with
wrapping and looping stitches. (W-30, L-17)*

INTERLACING STITCHES

No.	Foundation	Names	Directions	Diagrams	Stitch
I-1	warp	**interlacing stitch** weaving darning stitch cloth stitch	Work weft-wise from right to left. 1. The needle goes under warp 5, over warp 4, under warp 3, over warp 2, under warp 1.	**1.**　　**2.**	**I-1**
I-2	fabric	**interlacing stitch** running stitch	Work weft-wise from right to left. 1. Come out at a. Go in at b — out at c — in at d — out at e — in at f — out at g.	**1.**　　**2.**	**I-2**
I-3	stitches on fabric	**interlacing stitch** weaving stitch detached darning surface darning	The stitch works weft-wise from right to left. 1. Stitch A, B, C, D, and E on the fabric. (W-14) Come out of the fabric at a. The needle goes under stitch E, over stitch D, under stitch C, over stitch B, under stitch A. 2. Go into the fabric at b.	**1.**　　**2.**	**I-3**
I-4	warp floats stitches on fabric	**interlacing** weaving plain weave tabby	Work weft-wise from left to right. See I-1 for the first row of the stitch. 1. The needle goes over warp 1, under warp 2, over warp 3, under warp 4, over warp 5. (See Project Two)	**1.**	**I-4**

No.	Foundation	Names	Directions	Diagrams	Stitch
I-5	warp floats stitches on fabric	**interlacing** weaving balanced plain weave tabby	The diagram shows a sample of interlaced fabric in a balanced plain weave. Both warps and wefts alternate between dark and light elements to show the structure. A one inch square will have an equal number of ends (warps) per inch and picks (wefts) per inch. Works weft-wise right to left, left to right. 1. Follow the directions for I-1 and I-4. (See Project Two)		I-5
I-6	warp floats stitches on fabric	**interlacing** weft-faced plain weave tapestry	The diagram shows a sample of a weft-faced or tapestry weave. Because of the spacing of the warp the weft elements beat down to cover the warp. 1. Follow the directions for I-1 and I-4. (See Project Two)		I-6
I-7	warp	**interlacing** weaving warp-faced weaving warp-faced plain weave	The diagram shows a sample of a warp-faced weave. When the warps are very closely set and the weft pulled snug, the warps will cover the weft elements. Works weft-wise right to left, left to right. 1. Follow the directions for I-1, and I-4. (See Project Two)		I-7
I-8	warp floats stitches on fabric	**interlacing** weaving basket weave extended tabby	The diagram shows a sample of a basket weave—two warp threads and two weft threads interlacing. Works right to left, left to right. 1. Work with a double weft thread and interlace over and under warp pairs. Follow the directions for I-1 and I-4. (See Project Two)		I-8

No.	Foundation	Names	Directions	Diagrams	Stitch
I-9	warp floats stitches on fabric	**interlacing** weaving twill weave	The diagram shows a sample of a twill weave. 1. First pick: (from right to left) Begin with the bottom row. Go over 4, under 3 & 2, over 1 & 4, under 3 & 2, over 1. 2. Second pick: (from left to right) Go under 1 & 2, over 3 & 4, under 1 & 2, over 3 & 4. 3. Third Pick: (from right to left) Go under 4, over 3 & 2, under 1 & 4, over 3 & 2, under 1. 4. Fourth pick: (from left to right) Go over 1 & 2, under 3 & 4, over 1 & 2, under 3 & 4. (See Project Two)		**I-9**
I-10	warp floats stitches on fabric	**interlacing** Spanish lace Spanish openwork	This interlacing on a small set of warps is spaced to create openwork weaving. 1. Interlace over and under three warps for three picks, then move to the next set of three and repeat. Any number of warps may be in the set.		**I-10**
I-11	warp	**interlacing** tapestry slit tapestry weft-faced plain weave	Interlacing on small sets of warps is used in tapestry weaving to build adjacent color areas. A slit is left where the two colors wrap adjacent warps as they go back and forth. 1. Work with two weft colors and interlace on adjacent sets on warps.		**I-11**
I-12	warp	**interlacing** tapestry tapestry join	When the two wefts wrap around a common warp the color areas are joined. The wraps may be random or in a regular pattern. 1. Work with two weft colors and interlace on adjacent sets of warp. After several picks wrap the wefts around a common warp.		**I-12**

No.	Foundation	Names	Directions	Diagrams	Stitch
I-13	warp	weft-loop weave	An interlaced weft may be pulled where it passes over a warp to form a weft-loop. Works weft-wise from right to left. 1. Interlace a weft. Each weft-loop may be picked up on a knitting needle, or pulled out with a needle. 2. The rows of weft-loops should alternate with picks of plain interlacing for stability.	1. 2.	I-13
I-14	warp floats warp and woven fabric stitches on fabric	twining weft-twined weave	Two wefts that interlace and also cross one another between each warp pair form twining. Two wefts may be worked simultaneously or as described below. Work weft-wise from right to left. 1. Interlace the white weft. 2. The needle goes under warp 5 and the weft. 3. The needle goes under warp 3 and the weft. Continue across. See Project 7 for working twining at the loom.	1. 2. 3.	I-14
I-15	warp floats stitches on fabric	twill twining	Two wefts that interlace, cross one another, and also follow a twill sequence form twill twining. 1. Follow the directions for I-9 and I-14. Interlace over and under warp pairs. 2. The needle with the second weft goes over and under the opposite pairs of warps. See Project 7 for twill twining at the loom.	1. 2.	I-15
I-16	warp	Danish medallion	Interlaced patterns that pull together several weft picks are used in openwork weaves and called 'Danish medallions'. Work weft-wise from right to left. 1. Pick 1 and pick 4 would usually be the same color, the same weft brought up after two or three picks of another color. Interlace over and under a set of warps, pass the weft warp-wise under the picks, over a warp, and pass again under the picks leaving a small open loop in the weft. 2. Slip the weft through the open loop. Resume interlacing over and under the next set of warps.	1. 2.	I-16

No.	Foundation	Names	Directions	Diagrams	Stitch
I-17	warp		Another way to pull together several weft picks to form patterns is to use a knotting stitch Work weft-wise from right to left. 1. Follow the interlacing pattern I-16. Stitch a knot (K-1) upon a weft several picks below the working weft. Pull snug to group the wefts to form patterns of openwork. **1.**		**I-17**
I-18	floats stitches on fabric		A pair of looping stitches may be worked upon a foundation of weft floats or upon a row of stitches upon fabric with a second stitching element. Work weft-wise from left to right. 1. Interlace two picks of tabby and one pick with weft floats, then with another element work a pair of looping stitches (L-1) upon each float. **1.**		**I-18**
I-19	floats stitches on fabric		A pair of looping stitches may be worked upon a foundation of weft floats or a row of stitches upon fabric with a second stitching element. Work weft-wise from left to right. 1. Interlace two picks of tabby and one pick with weft floats, then with another element work a pair of looping stitches (L-33) upon each float or stitch. **1.**		**I-19**
I-20	floats stitches on fabric	Pekinese stitch forbidden stitch	A stitching element can work upon weft floats, warp floats or more typically a row of stitches on fabric (W-15) forming a pattern of wraps. Work weft-wise from left to right. 1. Slip the needle up under stitch B. 2. Slip the needle down under stitch A. Continue by slipping up under stitch C, down under stitch B. **1.** **2.**		**I-20**

No.	Foundation	Names	Directions	Diagrams	Stitch
I-21	floats stitches on fabric	guilloche stitch	One stitching element may work back and forth, or two stitching elements may work upon sets of floats or stitches to form a pattern. The dark stitching element works weft-wise from left to right. 1. The needle slips up under set A, down under set B, up under set C.	**1.** **2.**	I-21
I-22	warp floats stitches on fabric	gauze leno	A weft that interlaces and also fixes the warps in a crossed position forms a structure called gauze or leno. Work weft-wise from right to left. 1. Slip the needle under warp 3 from left to right. 2. Slip the needle under warp 4 from right to left. 3. Repeat these two motions on the 1 & 2 warp elements. See Project 7 for how to use a pick-up stick to hold the crossed warps.	**1.** **2.**	I-22
I-23	gauze fabric		The crossed warps of the gauze weave may work as a foundation for interlacing. The interlacing tends to be weft-faced. Work weft-wise from right to left; left to right. 1. Interlace over and under the crossed warps between picks of gauze and interlacing.	**1.**	I-23
I-24	radiating warp	**interlacing** weaving	The diagram shows a sample of interlacing on radiating warps. Work clockwise from the center to the outside of the circle. 1. Interlace over and under the spokes working clockwise. (The number of spokes must be uneven.)		I-24

No.	Foundation	Names	Directions	Diagrams	Stitch
I-25	radiating stitches on fabric	**interlacing** woven spider web	Radiating elements or radiating stitches on fabric may be knotted at the center and then interlaced with a stitching element. See W-66 for the foundation stitches and the knot. Work clockwise from the center to the outside of the circle. 1. Interlace over spoke a, under spoke b, over spoke c. 2. Interlace under spoke d, over spoke e. Continue around. (The number of spokes must be uneven.)	**1.** **2.**	I-25

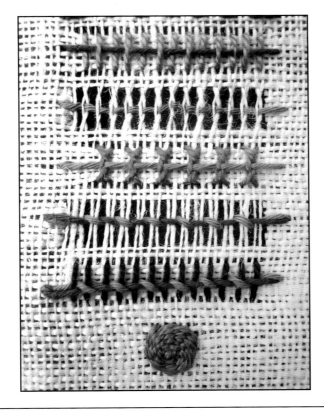

Figure 135: Interlacing stitches.

WRAPPING STITCHES

No.	Foundation	Names	Directions	Diagrams	Stitch
W-1	warp	**wrapping stitch** weft-wrap weave weft-wrapping Soumak	Work weft-wise from left to right. 1. The needle slips under warp 1 from right to left. 2. The needle slips under warp 2 from right to left. Continue across the warps. The needle works above the stitching element.		**W-1**
W-2	fabric	**wrapping stitch** stem stitch	Work weft-wise left to right. 1. Come out at a. Go in at b — out at c. 2. Go in at d — back out at b. Continue across the row. The needle works above the stitching element.		**W-2**
W-3	stitches on fabric	**wrapping stitch** raised stem stitch	Work weft-wise from left to right. 1. Follow W-14 for the stitches on fabric. Come out of the fabric at a. The needle slips under stitch A from right to left. 2. The needle slips under stitch B from right to left. Continue across the row. Go back into the fabric at b. The needle works above the stitching element.		**W-3**
W-4	warp stitches on fabric floats	**wrapping stitch** weft-wrapping Soumak single Soumak Swedish knot	Work weft-wise from right to left. 1. The needle slips under warp 4 from left to right. 2. The needle slips under warp 3 from left to right. The needle works below the stitching element.		**W-4**

No.	Foundation	Names	Directions	Diagrams	Stitch
W-5	fabric	**wrapping stitch**	Work weft-wise from right to left. 1. Come out at a. Go in at b — out at c. 2. Go in at d — back out at b. Continue across the row.	**1.** **2.**	**W-5**
W-6	warp floats stitches on fabric	**wrapping stitch** weft-wrapping countered weft-wrapping Soumak	Work weft-wise from right to left. The slant of the stitch will be the same as W-1, the opposite of W-4. 1. The needle slips under warp 4 from left to right. 2. The needle slips under warp 3 from left to right. The needle works above the stitching element.	**1.** **2.**	**W-6**
W-7	warp floats stitches on fabric		Work weft-wise from left to right across a set of warp. Each stitch wraps around a warp and splits through the stitching element. 1. Slip the needle under warp 1 from right to left and at the same time split through the stitching element. 2. Slip the needle under warp 2 from right to left and at the same time split through the stitching element.	**1.** **2.**	**W-7**
W-8	fabric	split stitch	Work weft-wise from left to right. 1. Come out at a. Go in at b — out at c and at the same time split through the stitching element. 2. Go in at d — out at e and at the same time split through the stitching element.	**1.** **2.**	**W-8**

No.	Foundation	Names	Directions	Diagrams	Stitch
W-9	single warp floats stitches on fabric	wrapping	Work warp-wise upon a single warp. 1. The needle slips from right to left behind warp 1. 2. The needle slips again behind warp 1. Continue wrapping around the warp.	**1.** **2.**	W-9
W-10	fabric	satin stitch	Work warp-wise upon fabric. 1. Come out at a. Go in at b — out at c. 2. Go in at d — out at e. Continue. The stitch will work warp-wise and weft-wise from either direction.	**1.** **2.**	W-10
W-11	fabric edge	overcast edge	Work warp-wise on a fabric edge. 1. Come out at a. Go under the edge of the fabric and come out at b.	**1.**	W-11
W-12	warp	wrapping	Work warp-wise from bottom to top. 1. Position the stitching element as in 1. 2. Work the wrapping stitches around the warp and the looped portion of the element. 3. The needle goes inside the loop at the top of the wrapping stitches. Pull down on the beginning portion of the stitching element. This will pull the working end inside the wraps and tighten the wraps. Both ends of the stitching element may be clipped.	**1.** **2.** **3.**	W-12

No.	Foundation	Names	Directions	Diagrams	Stitch
W-13	wrapped warps		Interlacing (I-1, I-4) may be worked upon a foundation of wrapped warps. See fig. 89 and 90.	**1.**	**W-13**
W-14	fabric	straight stitches	Work weft-wise from right to left to make a set of foundation stitches. (This is the same stitch as W-10, but spaced, and turned 90 degrees.) 1. Come out at a. Go in at b — out at c. In at d — out at e. In at f — out at g. In at h — out at i. In at j. 2. The stitches form stitch A, B, C, D, and E for foundation stitches on fabric.	j h f d / b ... A B C D E i g e c a **1.** **2.**	**W-14**
W-15	warp floats stitches on fabric	weft-wrapping Brook's Bouquet	Work weft-wise from right to left. This stitch is the reverse face of W-1 or W-4. Either the obverse or reverse of a wrapping stitch can be on the working surface. 1. Slip the needle under warp 4 from right to left. 2. Slip the needle again under warp 4 and also under warp 3. Continue across each time wrapping back around a warp and forward under the next warp to the left.	1 2 3 4 3 4 **1.** **2.**	**W-15**
W-16	fabric	back stitch	Work weft-wise from right to left. 1. Come out at a. Go in at b — out at c. 2. Go back in at a — out at d. Continue across the row. Each stitch goes back into the fabric where the last stitch ended.	c a b d c a **1.** **2.**	**W-16**

No.	Foundation	Names	Directions	Diagrams	Stitch
W-17	fabric	tent stitch continental stitch	Work weft-wise from right to left upon a fabric with open meshes. 1. The stitch works in and out of the open spaces in the weave. Compare with W-62, W-63.	**1.** **2.**	**W-17**
W-18	warp floats stitches on fabric	**wrapping stitch** Ceylon stitch knit-stem stitch cross-knit loop stitch loop stitch Peruvian needle knitting	Work weft-wise from left to right. 1. This is the same stitch as W-1, but do not pull the stitch tight to the warp. 2. Each stitch should be slightly loose. 3. The second row of stitches works upon the first row. Slip the needle horizontally behind the x formed by each wrapping stitch.	**1.** **2.** **3.**	**W-18**
W-19	warp floats stitches on fabric	**wrapping stitch** Ceylon stitch knit-stem stitch cross-knit loop stitch loop stitch Peruvian needle knitting	The same stitch will work with the x above the row of stitching.	**1.**	**W-19**
W-20	single warp ring	**wrapping stitch** Ceylon stitch knit-stem stitch cross-knit loop stitch loop stitch	Work warp-wise upon a single warp from bottom to top, or could be turned 90 degrees. 1. Works the same as W-9, except that the stitch is not pulled to the warp. 2. The needle slips from right to left under the warp. 3. The second row of stitches works upon the x formed by each stitch in the row above. (L-8 shows how to begin with a first row of looping stitches. L-12 upon a ring.)	**1.** **2.** **3.**	**W-20**

No.	Foundation	Names	Directions	Diagrams	Stitch
W-21	fabric	**wrapping stitch** Ceylon stitch	Work weft-wise from left to right. The stitch will also work around and around in a circle to form a tubular fabric. 1. Come out of the fabric at a. Go in at b — out at c. 2. Go in at d — out at e. Leave some slack in the stitch. 3. The second row of stitches works upon the x formed by each stitch in the row above.	1. 2. 3.	W-21
W-22	fabric	Van Dyke stitch	Work a row of warp-wise stitches from top to bottom. 1. Come out at a. Go in at b — out at c. 2. Go in at d — out at e. Slip behind the x formed by the first stitch from right to left. Continue down the row.	1. 2.	W-22
W-23	fabric edges	Van Dyke stitch	Work warp-wise between two fabric edges from top to bottom. 1. Come out at a. Go in at b, under the fabric edges — out at c. 2. Go in at d under the fabric edges — out at e. Slip behind the x formed by the first stitch from right to left.	1. 2.	W-23
W-24	fabric	ladder stitch	Work warp-wise from top to bottom. 1. Come out at a. Go in at b — out at c. Move to the right go in at d — out at e. Go in at f — out at g. Slip the needle from right to left behind the x formed by the first stitch. (a-b-c) 2. Slip the needle from right to left behind the x formed by the second stitch (d-e-f). Go in at h. Continue down the row of stitches.	1. 2.	W-24

No.	Foundation	Names	Directions	Diagrams	Stitch
W-25	fabric edges	ladder stitch	Work warp-wise between two edges of fabric from top to bottom. 1. Follow the instructions for W-24.	**1.** **2.**	W-25
W-26	fabric		Work warp-wise from top to bottom. 1. Come out at a. Go in at b — out at c. 2. Slip under the stitch a-b from right to left. 3. Go in at d. Come out at e. Slip under the right leg of the first stitch from right to left. Go in at f. Continue down the row.	**1.** **2.** **3.**	W-26
W-27	fabric edge		Work along a fabric edge. 1. Come out at a. Slip the needle under the edge of the fabric and come out at b. 2. Slip the needle from right to left under the first stitch. 3. Slip the needle under the edge of the fabric and come out at c. Continue this sequence.	**1.** **2.** **3.**	W-27
W-28	warp	linking	Work warp-wise upon a single warp, or could be turned 90 degrees. 1. When the wrap is spaced it can work as the foundation for a second row of wraps taken on the 'lag'. This structure forms net-like fabrics. A 'lag' is that loose portion of an element between two stitches.	**1.** **2.** **3.**	W-28

No.	Foundation	Names	Directions	Diagrams	Stitch
W-29	single element or multiple element bundle	coiling	The foundation element is wrapped and also attached to itself in a coiling or spiral pattern. 'Coiled baskets' are formed this way. 1. The wraps go around the foundation element and also attach to the previous row in a variety of ways—wrapping around two coils, or splitting through the previous coil or stitch.	1. 2.	W-29
W-30	warp pair floats stitches on fabric	needle weaving	Work between a pair of warps alternately wrapping from bottom to top. 1. Slip the needle under warp 1 from right to left. 2. Slip the needle under warp 2 from left to right. 3. Slip the needle under warp 1 from right to left. Repeat this sequence.	1. 2. 3.	W-30
W-31	fabric edges	antique seam	Work between two fabric edges from bottom to top. 1. Come out at a. Go under the edge of the left fabric and come out at b. 2. Go under the right fabric edge and come out at c. 3. Go under the left fabric edge and come out at d. Repeat this sequence.	1. 2. 3.	W-31
W-32	fabric edges	antique seam	Work between two fabric edges from bottom to top. 1. Works as above except the stitches are slanted. (W-31)		W-32

No.	Foundation	Names	Directions	Diagrams	Stitch
W-33	warp floats stitches on fabric		Work weft-wise from left to right in an alternating wrapping pattern. 1. Slip the needle from right to left under warp 1. The needle should come out *below* the stitching element. 2. Slip the needle under warp 2 from right to left. The needle should come out *above* the stitching element. Continue this pattern across the row.		W-33
W-34	fabric	alternating stem stitch	Work weft-wise from left to right. 1. Come out at a. Go in at b — out at c with the needle coming out *below* the stitching element. 2. Go in at d — back out at b with the needle coming out *above* the stitching element. Continue this alternating sequence across the row.		W-34
W-35	warp floats stitches on fabric	Turkish-knot Ghiordes-knot rya	Work weft-wise from left to right across a set of warps, alternately wrapping and leaving weft-loops. This is the same stitch as W-33 except that weft-loops are formed with alternate stitches. The weft-loops may be cut for a weft-pile. 1. Follow the directions for W-33, steps 1 and 2, but leave a weft-loop as in 3.		W-35
W-36	fabric	looped alternating stem stitch turkey work	Work weft-wise from left to right upon fabric. This is the same stitch as W-34 except that weft-loops are formed with the alternate stitch. The weft-loops may be cut for a weft-pile. 1. Follow the directions for W-34, steps 1 and 2, but leave a weft-loop as in 3.		W-36

No.	Foundation	Names	Directions	Diagrams	Stitch
W-37	warp	Turkish-knot Ghiordes-knot rya	A rod or stick may be used to keep the weft-loops the same size when worked upon either warp or fabric.	**1.**	**W-37**
W-38	warp floats stitches on fabric	Turkish-knot Ghiordes-knot rya	Pre-cut lengths of yarn can be wrapped around warp pairs to form the same structure.		**W-38**
W-39	fabric	rya stitch	Pre-cut lengths of yarn can be stitched on fabric for a fringe.		**W-39**
W-40	fabric	herringbone	Work weft-wise from left to right. 1. Come out at a. Go in at b — out at c. 2. Go in at d — out at e. 3. Go in at f — out at g.	**1.** **2.** **3.**	**W-40**

No.	Foundation	Names	Directions	Diagrams	Stitch
W-41	fabric edges	herringbone	Work between two fabric edges from left to right. 1. Follow the directions for W-40.		W-41
W-42	warp floats stitches on fabric		Work weft-wise from left to right. 1. Follow the directions for W-33 for step 1. Slip the needle under warp 3 from right to left. Come out *below* the stitching element. 2. Slip the needle under warp 4 from right to left and *above* the stitching element. 3. Slip the needle under warp 5 from right to left. Be sure with each pass of the needle that you are on the correct side of the stitching element.		W-42
W-43	fabric	chevron stitch	Work weft-wise from left to right. 1. Come out at a. Go in at b — out at c. 2. Go in at d — back out at b. Come out *below* the stitching element. 3. Go in at e — out at f. 4. Go in at g — out at e. Come out *above* the stitching element.		W-43
W-44	fabric edges	chevron stitch	Work from left to right between two fabric edges. Follow the directions for W-43.		W-44

No.	Foundation	Names	Directions	Diagrams	Stitch
W-45	warp floats stitches on fabric		Work weft-wise from right to left. 1. Slip the needle under warp 4 from right to left. 2. Slip the needle again under warp 4 from right to left. 3. Slip the needle under both warp 4 and 3. Each warp will be wrapped twice.		W-45
W-46	fabric		Work weft-wise from right to left. 1. Come out at a. Go in at b — out at c. 2. Go in at d — out at e. 3. Go back in at c — out at f. Go back in at a — out at g. Repeat this sequence.		W-46
W-47	fabric edges		Work between two fabric edges. 1. Follow the directions for W-46.		W-47
W-48	fabric or fabric edge	velvet stitch	Work weft-wise from right to left to form a stitch with loops. 1. Come out at a. Go in at b — out at c. Leave an open loop of the stitching element between a and b. 2. Go back in at b — back out at a. 3. Go in at d. Repeat the sequence to the left of the first stitch. The loops can be cut for a pile or fringe.		W-48

No.	Foundation	Names	Directions	Diagrams	Stitch
W-49	warp and woven fabric	hemming stitch	Work weft-wise from right to left to hem woven fabric. The stitch wraps around warp pairs and then through the fabric. (The weft is used as the stitching element.) 1. The needle slips under the warp pair at the right. 2. The needle slips under the warp pair at the right again and comes out two weft picks above. 3. Repeat the wrapping sequence across the warp pairs.	1.　　2.　　3.	W-49
W-50	warp floats stitches on fabric		Work weft-wise across a set of warps from left to right. A wrap and a looping stitch are worked upon each stitch. 1. Slip the needle under warp 1 from right to left. 2. Slip the needle down under the first portion of the stitch. 3. Slip the needle again down under the first portion of the stitch and *over* the looped portion of the stitching element. Repeat the sequence on the next warp to the right.	1.　　2.　　3.	W-50
W-51	fabric	Palestrina Knot	Work weft-wise from left to right. 1. Come out at a. Go in at b — out at c. 2. Slip the needle down under stitch a-b. 3. Slip the needle down under stitch a-b again and come out *over* the looped portion of the stitching element.	1.　　2.　　3.	W-51
W-52	single element float stitches on fabric	Lace stitch filling Tulle stitch double tulle stitch loop and twist Spanish Point	Work from left to right upon a single element weft-wise or warp-wise. 1. Position the stitching element as in 1. Slip the needle under the foundation element from top to bottom. 2. A second row of stitching works upon the first row. (The stitch is a wrapping stitch with a wrap, and can be formed with those two motions.)	1.　　2.	W-52

No.	Foundation	Names	Directions	Diagrams	Stitch
W-53	fabric		Work weft-wise from left to right. 1. Come out at a. Position the stitching element as in 1. Go in at b — out at c. 2. Repeat the sequence at d and e.	**1.** **2.**	W-53
W-54	fabric edge		Work along a fabric edge from left to right. 1. Come out at a. Position the stitching element as in 1. Go in at b and come out under the edge of the fabric. 2. Repeat the sequence.	**1.** **2.**	W-54
W-55	warp pair floats stitches on fabric		Work warp-wise from bottom to top between two warps. 1. Slip the needle under warp 1 from right to left, then under the first portion of the stitching element as in 1. 2. Slip the needle under warp 2 from left to right. 3. Slip the needle down under the portion of the stitching element as in 3.	**1.** **2.** **3.**	W-55
W-56	fabric edges	faggoting	Work between two fabric edges from bottom to top. 1. Come out at a. Slip under the edge of the left fabric and come out at b. Slip the needle under the stitch from a to b. 2. Go under the edge of the right fabric and come out at c. Slip the needle under the stitch from b to c. Repeat these two stitches.	**1.** **2.** **3.**	W-56

No.	Foundation	Names	Directions	Diagrams	Stitch
W-57	warp	wrapped twining weft-twining with a full twist Taaniko twining	A rigid or flexible element may be laid across the reverse of the warp and a second element wrap around that element between warp pairs. Work weft-wise from left to right. 1. Lay an element across the reverse of the warp. The needle slips under that element as in 1. Repeat the wrap between each warp pair. (If both elements are flexible they may exchange positions for color changes.)	 1.	W-57
W-58	warp	weft-wrapping supplementary weft-wrapping with tapestry	Wrapping stitches combine with tapestry weaves (I-6) to outline areas, change surface textures, to draw details, and to create patterns.		W-58
W-59	warp	weft-wrapping supplementary weft-wrapping with tapestry	Wrapping stitches can work warp-wise or diagonally to outline a tapestry area. (See fig. 68, 70 and plate 2.)		W-59
W-60	warp	weft-wrapping supplementary weft-wrapping with tapestry	The wrapping element can float over picks of interlaced wefts to outline, draw, or form patterns.		W-60

No.	Foundation	Names	Directions	Diagrams	Stitch
W-61	warp	weft-wrapping Supplementary weft-wrapping with tapestry	Two or more wrapping elements can float over picks of interlaced wefts to form patterns.		**W-61**
W-62	gauze fabric		Wrapping stitches may be worked upon a gauze fabric foundation; the open meshes in the fabric used as one would use a needlepoint canvas. 1. Follow I-32 for the gauze fabric. 2. Follow W-17 for the stitch. See fig. 53, 54, and 55.	 **1.** **2.**	**W-62**
W-63	gauze fabric		1. Follow I-32 for the gauze fabric. 2. Follow W-10 for the stitch.	 **1.**	**W-63**
W-64	cruciform elements stitches on fabric	God's eye	Work clockwise upon cruciform elements. 1. Attach the stitching element to the center of the cross. Work a wrapping stitch (W-1) around each arm of the cross.	 **1.** **2.** **3.**	**W-64**

No.	Foundation	Names	Directions	Diagrams	Stitch
W-65	cruciform elements stitches on fabric	God's eye	Work clockwise upon cruciform elements. 1. Attach the stitching element to the center of the cross. Work wrapping stitch (W-15) around each arm of the cross.	**1.** **2.** **3.**	W-65
W-66	radiating elements		Work a set of radiating elements that are rigid or stretched across a circular frame. 1. The radiating elements. 2. Attach the stitching element at the center of the radiating elements with a knotting stitch.	**1.** **2.**	W-66
W-67	radiating stitches on fabric		Work a set of stitches that span a circle. 1. Follow the letters and work the three stitches that cross in the center of the circle. Come out at g. 2. Stitch a knotting stitch around the center of the stitches.	**1.** **2.**	W-67
W-68	radiating elements stitches on fabric	raised stem spider web	Work clockwise around the circle with a wrapping stitch. (W-1) 1. (Follow W-66 or W-67 to begin.) Slip the needle under spoke d. 2. Slip the needle under spoke b. Continue around the spokes. Each stitch will wrap around a spoke.	**1.** **2.**	W-68

No.	Foundation	Names	Directions	Diagrams	Stitch
W-69	radiating elements radiating stitches on fabric	whipped spider web ribbed spider web	Work clockwise around the circle with a wrapping stitch. (W-15) (Follow W-58 or W-59 to begin.) 1. Slip the needle under spokes d and b. 2. Slip the needle back around spoke b and under e. Continue the sequence each time wrapping the last spoke and going under the next one clockwise.	**1.** **2.**	**W-69**

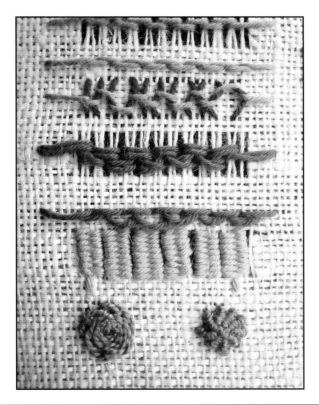

Figure 136: Wrapping stitches.

LOOPING STITCHES

No.	Foundation	Names	Directions	Diagrams	Stitch
L-1	warp	**looping stitch** buttonhole stitch	Work weft-wise from left to right. 1. The needle slips from left to right under warp 1 and then *over* the stitching element. 2. The needle slips from left to right under warp 2 and then *over* the stitching element. Repeat this sequence on each warp.	**1.** **2.**	**L-1**
L-2	fabric	**looping stitch** buttonhole stitch blanket stitch	Work weft-wise from left to right. 1. Come out at a. Go in at b — out at c and *over* the stitching element. The needle may enter at a slant or b and c could be at right angles to a. 2. Go in at d — out at c and *over* the stitching element. Repeat this sequence.	**1.** **2.**	**L-2**
L-3	stitches on fabric	**looping stitch** buttonhole stitch	Work weft-wise from left to right. See W-14 for the foundation stitches. 1. Come out of the fabric at a. The needle slips from left to right under stitch A and comes *over* the stitching element. 2. The needle slips from left to right under stitch B and comes over the stitching element. Go back into the fabric at b.	**1.** **2.**	**L-3**
L-4	fabric edge	**looping stitch** buttonhole stitch blanket stitch	Work weft-wise from left to right on a fabric edge. 1. Come out at a. Go in at b — come out under the edge of the fabric and *over* the stitching element. 2. Go in at c — come out under the edge of the fabric and *over* the stitching element.	**1.** **2.**	**L-4**

No.	Foundation	Names	Directions	Diagrams	Stitch
L-5	warp floats stitches on fabric	**looping stitch** buttonhole stitch	Work weft-wise from right to left. 1. The needle slips from right to left under warp 4 and *over* the stitching element. 2. The needle slips from right to left under warp 3 and *over* the stitching element. Repeat this sequence on each warp.	**1.** **2.**	L-5
L-6	fabric	**looping stitch** buttonhole stitch blanket stitch	Work weft-wise from right to left. 1. Come out at a. Go in at b — out at c and *over* the stitching element. 2. Go in at d — out at e and *over* the stitching element. Repeat the sequence.	**1.** **2.**	L-6
L-7	warp and woven fabric	**looping stitch** buttonhole stitch	Work weft-wise from right to left upon warp pairs and woven fabric. 1. The weft is threaded through the needle to work as the stitching element. Slip the needle between weft 2 and 3 as it wraps around the outer warp at the right, come out below the bottom weft, under a warp pair, and *over* the stitching element. 2. Work the same stitch on the next warp pair to the left.	**1.** **2.**	L-7
L-8	single warp float single stitch on fabric	**looping stitch** detached buttonhole stitch half-hitch	Work warp-wise from bottom to top. 1. The needle slips from left to right under warp 1 and *over* the stitching element. 2. The needle slips from left to right under the warp and *over* the stitching element. 3. The looping stitches may be spaced. 4. The looping stitches may be close.	**1.** **2.** **3.** **4.**	L-8

No.	Foundation	Names	Directions	Diagrams	Stitch
L-9	row of stitches	**looping stitch** detached buttonhole knot-less netting buttonhole net stitch	Work warp-wise upon a row of looping stitches. 1. The second row of looping stitches works upon the 'lag' between the two stitches. The needle slips under the lag from left to right and *over* the stitching element. The stitches can be spaced or close.	**1.**	L-9
L-10	single element float stitch on fabric	**looping stitch** detached buttonhole stitch half-hitch	Work weft-wise from left to right. 1. The needle slips under the single element from top to bottom and over the stitching element. 2. The needle slips under the single element from top to bottom and over the stitching element. 3. The second row works upon the lags between the looping stitches of the first row. Stitches may be spaced or close.	**1.** **2.** **3.**	L-10
L-11	fabric row of stitches on fabric	**looping stitch** buttonhole stitch	Work weft-wise from left to right. The first row upon the fabric, the second row upon the first row of stitches. 1. Come out at a. Go in at b — out at c and over the stitching element. 2. The second row of stitches does not go into the fabric, but works upon the lags between the stitches of the first row. Come out at s, slip the needle under the lag and over the stitching element.	**1.** **2.**	L-11
L-12	ring	**looping stitch** half-hitch	Work counter-clockwise around a ring shaped element. 1. The needle slips under the ring and over the stitching element. 2. The needle slips under the ring and over the stitching element. The stitches may be spaced or close, a tubular fabric formed.	**1.** **2.**	L-12

No.	Foundation	Names	Directions	Diagrams	Stitch
L-13	row of stitches	**looping stitch** detached buttonhole stitch	Work from left to right and then from right to left, one row upon the last to form a fabric that is net or lace-like. 1. The first row works from left to right. The second row works from right to left. The needle slips under the lag and over the stitching element as in 1.	**1.**	L-13
L-14	fabric	detached chain stitch	Work to make a single closed looping stitch. 1. Come out at a. Go back in at a — out at b and over the stitching element. 2. Go back into the fabric at c. 3. The stitches can be arranged in radiating patterns. Begin the stitches at the outside of the circle. 4. The stitches begin at the center of the circle.	**1.** **2.** **3.** **4.**	L-14
L-15	fabric	fly stitch	Work to make a single open looping stitch. 1. Come out at a. Go in at b — out at c and over the stitching element. 2. Go back into the fabric at d.	**1.** **2.**	L-15
L-16	fabric edge		Work upon a fabric edge from left to right. 1. Come out at a. Go in at b — come out below the edge of the fabric and *over* the stitching element. (If the edge is formed by a fold the needle may slip between the two layers and out at the edge of the fold.) 2. Come out at c. Go in at d — come out under the edge of the fabric and *over* the stitching element.	**1.** **2.**	L-16

No.	Foundation	Names	Directions	Diagrams	Stitch
L-17	single warp float single stitch on fabric		Work warp-wise from top to bottom. 1. Stitch a looping stitch on the warp. 2. The needle slips inside the top of the first looping stitch, under the warp, and *over* the stitching element.	**1.** **2.**	L-17
L-18	fabric	square chain stitch	Work warp-wise from top to bottom. 1. Come out at a. Go in at b — out at c and *over* the stitching element. 2. As you go in at d hold the a-b-c portion of the first stitch to the right with the needle. Go in at d — out at e and *over* the stitching element. 3. The row of stitches is ended by going back into the fabric as at h.	**1.** **2.** **3.**	L-18
L-19	fabric edges	square chain stitch	Work warp-wise between two fabric edges from top to bottom. 1. Come out at a on the left fabric. Go in at b on the right fabric — out at c on the left fabric, and *over* the stitching element. 2. Go in at d — out at e with the needle holding the first stitch to the side.	**1.** **2.**	L-19
L-20	pair of warps floats stitches on fabric		Work warp-wise between two warps from top to bottom. The looping stitches alternate from side to side. 1. The needle slips from left to right under warp 1 and *over* the stitching element. 2. The needle slips from right to left under warp 2 and *over* the stitching element. 3. The stitches may be spaced. 4. The stitches may be close.	**1.** **2.** **3.** **4.**	L-20

No.	Foundation	Names	Directions	Diagrams	Stitch
L-21	fabric	feather stitch Cretan stitch	Work warp-wise from top to bottom. The looping stitches alternate from side to side. 1. Come out at a. Go in at b — out at c and *over* the stitching element. 2. Go in at d — out at e and *over* the stitching element. Notice that the needle changes direction on alternate stitches. The needle can also enter on the diagonal. 3. When the stitch is worked with different spacing, less fabric picked up from b-c and d-e, the stitch is called a Cretan stitch.	**L-21** **1.** **2.** **3.**	**L-21**
L-22	fabric edges		Work warp-wise between two fabric edges. 1. Come out at a. Go in at b — come out under the edge of the fabric and *over* the stitching element. 2. Go in at c — come out under the edge of the fabric and *over* the stitching element. 3. Go in at d — come out under the edge of the fabric and *over* the stitching element. The stitches may be spaced or close.	**L-22** **1.** **2.** **3.**	**L-22**
L-23	pair of warps floats stitches on fabric		Work warp-wise from bottom to top. 1. The needle slips from left to right under warp 1 and *over* the stitching element. 2. The needle slips from right to left under warp 2, and *over* the stitching element.	**L-23** **1.** **2.**	**L-23**
L-24	fabric		Work warp-wise upon fabric, the looping stitches alternating from side to side. 1. Come out at a. Go in at b — out at c and *over* the stitching element. 2. Go in at d — out at e and *over* the stitching element.	**L-24** **1.** **2.**	**L-24**

No.	Foundation	Names	Directions	Diagrams	Stitch
L-25	pair of warps floats stitches on fabric		Work warp-wise from top to bottom or from bottom to top. The looping stitches alternate in pairs upon the two warps.		**L-25**
L-26	fabric		Work warp-wise upon fabric. The looping stitches alternate in pairs from side to side. Two are worked on the right, two are worked on the left.		**L-26**
L-27	fabric edges		Work warp-wise between two fabric edges. The looping stitches are worked in pairs, two on the fabric on the right, two on the fabric on the left.		**L-27**
L-28	pair of warps floats stitches on fabric		Work warp-wise from top to bottom or from bottom to top upon a warp pair. The stitches alternate in sets of three upon the two warps.		**L-28**

No.	Foundation	Names	Directions	Diagrams	Stitch
L-29	fabric		Work warp-wise from top to bottom or from bottom to top. The looping stitches alternate in sets of three from side to side.		L-29
L-30	fabric edges		Work warp-wise between two fabric edges. The looping stitches are worked in sets of three: three on the fabric on the right, three on the fabric on the left.		L-30
L-31	warp floats stitches on fabric		Work weft-wise upon pairs of warps from left to right. 1. The needle slips from right to left under warp 2 and *over* the stitching element. 2. The needle slips from left to right under warp 1 and *over* the stitching element. 3. The needle slips from right to left under warp 3 and *over* the stitching element. Repeat this sequence on warp 2 and 4.	1. 2. 3.	L-31
L-32	warp floats stitches on fabric		Work weft-wise upon warp from left to right. 1. The needle slips from left to right under warp 1 and *over* the stitching element. 2. The needle slips from left to right under warp 2 and *over* the stitching element. 3. The needle slips from left to right under warp 3 and *over* the stitching element.	1. 2. 3.	L-32

No.	Foundation	Names	Directions	Diagrams	Stitch
L-33	single warp float stitch on fabric	cow hitch lark's head knot detached up and down buttonhole tatting knot	Works to form two looping stitches that are crossing in opposite directions.	1.　　　　2.	L-33
L-34	single element warp float stitch on fabric	detached up and down buttonhole stitch	Work pairs of looping stitches weft-wise from left to right upon a single element foundation. 1. The needle slips from top to bottom under the single element and over the stitching element to work a looping stitch. 2. The stitching element is positioned as in 2. The needle slips from bottom to top under the single element and over the stitching element. 3. Repeat steps 1 and 2. A second row of stitches is worked on the lags between the pairs of stitches in the first row.	1.　　　2.　　　3.	L-34
L-35	fabric	up and down buttonhole	Work weft-wise from left to right upon fabric. 1. Come out at a. Go in at b — out at c and *over* the stitching element. 2. Go back in at c — back out at b and *over* the stitching element that is positioned as in 2. 3. Repeat the sequence going in at d — out at e. Back in at e — back out at d and *over* the stitching element.	1.　　　2.　　　3.	L-35
L-36	fabric edge		Work weft-wise from left to right along a fabric edge. 1. Come out at a. Go in at b — come out under the fabric edge and *over* the stitching element. 2. Position the stitching element as in 2. Go under the edge of the fabric and come back out at b. 3. Go in at c and repeat the sequence.	1.　　　2.　　　3.	L-36

No.	Foundation	Names	Directions	Diagrams	Stitch
L-37	ring	tatting knot cow hitch lark's head knot	Work counter-clockwise around a ring shaped element. 1. The needle slips under the ring and over the stitching element. 2. Position the stitching element as in 2. The needle slips up under the ring and over the stitching element. The stitches may be spaced or close, a tubular fabric formed. 'Tatted' rings are worked in this stitch with a tatting shuttle.	L-37	L-37
L-38	fabric		Work weft-wise from left to right with alternating pairs of looping stitches. 1. Follow L-35 for the first stitch a-b-c. Go in at d — out at e and over the stitching element. 2. Go back in at e — back out at d and over the stitching element. 3. Go in at f — out at g. Repeat the sequence.	L-38	L-38
L-39	fabric edges		Work weft-wise between two fabric edges with alternating pairs of looping stitches. 1. Follow L-36 for the first stitch. Go in c — Come out under the edge of the fabric and over the stitching element. 2. Position the stitching element as in 2. Go under the edge of the fabric and out at c. Repeat steps 1 and 2.	L-39	L-39
L-40	pair of warps floats stitches on fabric		Work warp-wise from top to bottom between a pair of warps. 1. The needle slips from right to left under warp 2 and over the stitching element. 2. The needle slips from right to left under warp 1. 3. Repeat the sequence working one looping stitch on warp 2 and then a wrapping stitch on warp 1. The stitch may be spaced or close.	L-40	L-40

No.	Foundation	Names	Directions	Diagrams	Stitch
L-41	fabric	Roumanian stitch	Work warp-wise from top to bottom upon fabric. 1. Come out at a. Go in at b — out at c. 2. Go in at d — out at e. 3. Go in at f — out at g.	 1. 2. 3.	L-41
L-42	fabric edges	Roumanian Stitch	Work warp-wise from top to bottom between two fabric edges. 1. Come out at a. Go in at b — come out under the edge of the fabric and *over* the stitching element. 2. Go under the edge of the fabric and out at c. 3. Go in at d — come out under the edge of the fabric and *over* the stitching element.	 1. 2. 3.	L-42
L-43	single element float stitch on fabric		Work weft-wise from left to right upon a single element. The stitch combines a loop with a wrap. 1. The needle slips from top to bottom under the single element and over the stitching element. 2. The needle slips up under the lag of the stitch. 3. Repeat steps 1 and 2. A second row of stitches works upon the lags in the first row.	 1. 2.	L-43
L-44	fabric		Work weft-wise from left to right. 1. Come out at a. Go in at b — out at c. 2. The needle slips under the stitch a-b from bottom to top. 3. Go in at d — out at e. Wrap around the stitch.	 1. 2. 3.	L-44

No.	Foundation	Names	Directions	Diagrams	Stitch
L-45	fabric edge		Work weft-wise from left to right along a fabric edge. 1. Come out at a. Go in at b — come out under the edge of the fabric and *over* the stitching element. 2. The needle slips up under the first stitch a-b. Go in at c. Repeat the sequence.	**1.** **2.**	L-45
L-46	warp floats stitches on fabric	raised chain band	Work weft-wise from left to right. The stitch combines a wrap with a looping stitch. 1. The needle slips from right to left under warp 1. 2. The needle slips from left to right under warp 1 and *over* the stitching element. 3. Repeat the sequence on warp 2. The stitch may be spaced or close.	1 2 3 4 **1.** **2.** **3.**	L-46
L-47	fabric		Work weft-wise from left to right upon fabric. 1. Come out at a. Go in at b — out at c. 2. Go in at d — back out at b and over the stitching element. 3. Go in at e — out at f. Repeat the sequence.	**1.** **2.** **3.**	L-47
L-48	pair of warps floats stitches on fabric		Work warp-wise from top to bottom between two warps. 1. The stitching element wraps around warp 2. Work 3 looping stitches on the lag from right to left. 2. Wrap around warp 1. Work 3 looping stitches on the second lag from left to right.	**1.** **2.**	L-48

No.	Foundation	Names	Directions	Diagrams	Stitch
L-49	fabric edges	Italian buttonhole insertion	Work warp-wise from top to bottom between two fabric edges. 1. Come out at a. Go in at b — and come out under the edge of the fabric. Work three looping stitches on the stitch a-b. 2. Go in c — come out under the edge of the fabric. 3. Work three looping stitches from left to right on the lag. Repeat the sequence.	**1.** **2.** **3.**	**L-49**
L-50	single element float stitch on fabric	buttonhole bar with ring picot	Work weft-wise from left to right upon a single element. 1. Work a series of close looping stitches upon the single element. (L-8) The needle slips up under the lag of a stitch. 2. Work a series of looping stitches from left to right upon the 'ring'. You can continue working looping stitches on the single element after the 'ring' is filled with stitches.	**1.** **2.**	**L-50**
L-51	single element float stitch on fabric	buttonhole bar with bullion picot	Work weft-wise from left to right upon a single element. 1. Work a series of close looping stitches upon the single element. (L-8) The needle slips up through the looping stitch on the right. 2. Work a multiple wrapped knot upon the stitch. (K-25) (K-27) Continue working looping stitches along the single element.	**1.** **2.**	**L-51**
L-52	single element float stitch on fabric	knotted loop knotted buttonhole	Work weft-wise from left to right upon a single element. 1. Work a looping stitch upon the element. 2. Work a knotting stitch upon the looping stitch. The needle slips from left to right under the stitch and over the stitching element. 3. Repeat the sequence. A second row of knotted looping stitches works on the lags of the first row. The stitches can be spaced or close.	**1.** **2.** **3.**	**L-52**

No.	Foundation	Names	Directions	Diagrams	Stitch
L-53	fabric		Work weft-wise from left to right upon fabric. 1. Work a looping stitch. Come out at a. Go in at b — out at c coming over the stitching element. 2. Work a knotting stitch upon the looping stitch. The needle slips under the a-b stitch and over the stitching element. 3. Repeat the sequence.	 **1.** **2.** **3.**	**L-53**
L-54	fabric edge	Antwerp edging stitch	Work weft-wise from left to right along a fabric edge. 1. Come out at a. Go in at b — come out under the fabric edge and over the stitching element. 2. The needle slips under the looping stitch and over the stitching element to make a knotting stitch.	 **1.** **2.**	**L-54**
L-55	warp and woven fabric		Work weft-wise from left to right upon warp pairs and a woven edge. 1. Thread the weft end through the needle. Work a looping stitch as in 1, coming out between the first warp pair and over the stitching element. 2. The looping stitch. 3. Work a knotting stitch on the first pair of warps. Repeat the sequence on each pair of warps.	 **1.** **2.** **3.**	**L-55**
L-56	radiating elements radiating stitches on fabric		Work counter-clockwise around a set of radiating elements from the center to the outside. 1. Follow W-66 or W-67 to begin. Work a looping stitch (L-5) on spoke d. 2. Work a looping stitch on spoke f. (L-5) Continue working counter-clockwise around the circle.	 **1.** **2.**	**L-56**

CHAINING STITCHES

No.	Foundation	Names	Directions	Diagrams	Stitch
C-1	warp	**chaining stitch** chain stitch	Work weft-wise from left to right upon warp. 1. The first stitch is a looping stitch. (L-1) The first stitch could also be a knot. (K-4) 2. The needle goes *inside* the looping stitch, under warp 2, and over the stitching element. Each stitch repeats step 2, going *inside* the last stitch, under the warp, and over the stitching element.	**C-1**
C-2	fabric	**chaining stitch** chain stitch	Work weft-wise from left to right. 1. Come out at a. Go back in at a — out at b coming over the stitching element. 2. Go back in at b *inside* the first chain stitch — come out at c and over the stitching element.	**C-2**
C-3	stitches on fabric	**chaining stitch**	Work weft-wise from left to right. Follow W-14 for working the set of foundation stitches. 1. Come out of the fabric at a. Work a looping stitch on stitch A. 2. The needle goes *inside* the looping stitch, under stitch B, and over the stitching element. Remember to always go *inside* of the chain as well as under the warp and over the stitching element. Go back into the fabric at b.	**C-3**
C-4	warp floats stitches on fabric	**chaining stitch** chain stitch	Work weft-wise from right to left. 1. The first stitch on warp 4 is a looping stitch (L-5) or a knot (K-1). 2. Go *inside* the looping stitch on warp 4, under warp 3, and over the stitching element.	**C-4**

No.	Foundation	Names	Directions	Diagrams	Stitch
C-5	fabric	**chaining stitch** chain stitch	Work weft-wise from right to left. 1. Come out at a. Go back in at a — out at b coming over the stitching element. 2. Go back in at b *inside* the first stitch — come out at c and over the stitching element.	1. 2.	C-5
C-6	warp and woven fabric	**chaining stitch** chain stitch	Work weft-wise from right to left upon warp pairs and woven fabric. 1. Thread the needle with the weft. Work a looping stitch (L-5) or a knot (K-1) upon the first warp pair on the right. Then work chain stitches around each warp pair. The needle must go inside each stitch, under the warp pair and over the stitching element.		C-6
C-7	single element	chaining interlooping	Work with only the single element to form a continuous chain of stitches. 1. The element crosses itself. 2. The working end of the element passes under the crossed loop. 3. A 'bight' or 'loop' of the working element is pulled partially through. Each new chain stitch is a loop pulled partially through the last chain stitch. (A crochet hook may be used.)	1. 2. 3.	C-7
C-8	single element	chaining	Begin upon a single element then work a continuous chain of stitches. 1. The needle works a looping stitch (L-5) or a knotting stitch (K-1) upon an element. 2. The needle slips *inside* the stitch and over the stitching element to form a chain stitch. Each new chain stitch works back inside the last. (A crochet hook may be used.)	1. 2.	C-8

No.	Foundation	Names	Directions	Diagrams	Stitch
C-9	fabric	chaining	Begin with a stitch upon fabric and then work a continuous chain of stitches free of the fabric. 1. Work a looping stitch (l-14) or a knotting stitch (K-2) upon the fabric. 2. Work a series of chain stitches that do not go into the fabric. The needle works inside the last chain stitch and over the stitching element.	**1.** **2.**	C-9
C-10	warp floats stitches on fabric	**chaining stitch**	Work weft-wise from right to left. 1. The stitching element is laid weft-wise across the reverse of the warp. 2. A 'bight' or loop is pulled up between warp 3 and 4. 3. A 'bight' or loop is pulled up inside the first loop and in between warp 2 and 3. Repeat the sequence going *inside* the last chain stitch and between each warp pair for each new stitch.	**1.** **2.** **3.**	C-10
C-11	warp floats stitches on fabric	magic chain checkered chain band	Work with two stitching elements weft-wise from right to left. 1. Two stitching elements are threaded through the needle. First work a stitch with the light element on warp 2. Keep the dark element out of the way. 2. Work a chain stitch with the dark element on warp 1. Keep the light element out of the way. 3. Alternate the colors every other stitch.	**1.** **2.**	C-11
C-12	fabric	magic chain	Work weft-wise from right to left with a needle threaded with two elements. 1. Work the first stitch with the light element. Keep the dark element out of the way. 2. Work the second stitch with the dark element. Keep the light element out of the way. Continue the sequence.	**1.** **2.** **3.**	C-12

No.	Foundation	Names	Directions	Diagrams	Stitch
C-13	radiating elements radiating stitches on fabric		Work counter-clockwise around a set of radiating elements. 1. Follow W-66 or W-67 to begin. Work a looping stitch (L-1) upon spoke d. 2. Work a chaining stitch that goes inside of the last stitch, under spoke f, and out over the stitching element. Work each new stitch back inside the last stitch and under the warp. Continue around the circle.	**1.** **2.**	**C-13**

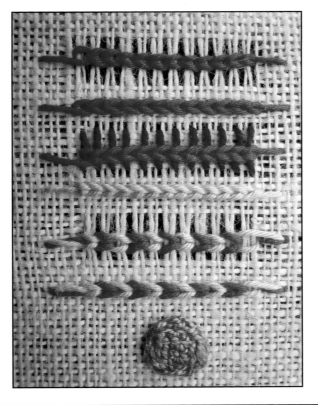

Figure 137: Chaining stitches.

KNOTTING STITCHES

No.	Foundation	Names	Directions	Diagrams	Stitch
K-1	warp	**knotting stitch** knotted weft-wrapping	Work weft-wise from right to left. 1. The needle slips under warp 4 and the stitching element and comes out over the looped portion of the stitching element. 2. The needle slips under warp 3 and the stitching element and comes out over the looped portion of the stitching element. Always remember to position the stitching element as in 1 and 2 or it will not form a knot.	**1.** **2.**	**K-1**
K-2	fabric	**knotting stitch** coral knot stitch twisted chain stitch	Work weft-wise from right to left. 1. Come out at a. Go in at b and under the stitching element — out at c and over the looped portion of the stitching element. 2. Go in at d and under the stitching element — come out at e and over the looped portion of the stitching element. Always remember to position the stitching element as in 1 and 2 or it will not form a knot.	**1.** **2.**	**K-2**
K-3	stitches on fabric	**knotting stitch**	Work weft-wise from right to left. 1. See W-14 for working the foundation stitches. Come out of the fabric at a. The needle slips under stitch D and under the stitching element and comes out over the looped portion of the stitching element. 2. The needle slips under stitch C — and comes out over the looped portion of the stitching element.	**1.** **2.**	**K-3**
K-4	warp floats stitches on fabric	**knotting stitch** knotted weft-wrapping	Work weft-wise from left to right. 1. The needle slips under warp 1 and under the stitching element and comes out over the looped portion of the stitching element. 2. The needle slips under warp 2 and under the stitching element and comes out over the looped portion of the stitching element.	**1.** **2.**	**K-4**

No.	Foundation	Names	Directions	Diagrams	Stitch
K-5	fabric	**knotting stitch** coral knot stitch twisted chain stitch	Work weft-wise from left to right. 1. Come out at a. Go in at b and under the stitching element — come out at c and over the looped portion of the stitching element. 2. Go in at d and under the stitching element — come out at e and over the looped portion of the stitching element.	**K-5**
K-6	warp	**knotting stitch**	Work weft-wise from right to left. The knob of the knot appears on the reverse side of the fabric when worked this way. 1. Slip a looped portion of the stitching element under warp 4. 2. The needle slips up under — and out over the looped portion of the stitching element. 3. Slip a looped portion of the stitching element under warp 3 and slip the needle through that for the next stitch.	**K-6**
K-7	single element	knot simple knot overhand knot	The single element works knots upon itself. 1. The needle slips through the crossed loop in the working element. 2. The needle slips through a second crossed loop in the working element.	**K-7**
K-8	single element	knot	The single element is worked into a knot with the hands.	**K-8**

No.	Foundation	Names	Directions	Diagrams	Stitch
K-9	fabric edges	**knotting stitch**	Work weft-wise from right to left. 1. Come out at a. Go in b under the edge of the fabric and under the stitching element — come out at c from under the edge of the fabric and go over the looped portion of the stitching element.	**1.**	K-9
K-10	fabric	**knotting stitch** twisted chain stitch rope stitch	Work warp-wise from top to bottom. 1. Come out at a. Go in at b and under the stitching element — out at c and over the looped portion of the stitching element. 2. Go in at d and under the stitching element — come out at e and over the looped portion of the stitching element. The stitch may be left open or pulled tight, the stitches close or spaced.	**1.** **2.** **3.**	K-10
K-11	fabric edge		Work warp-wise from top to bottom along a fabric edge. 1. Come out at a. The needle goes in under the edge of the fabric and under the stitching element — comes out at b and over the looped portion of the stitching element. 2. The needle slips under the edge of the fabric and under the stitching element — comes out at c and over the looped portion of the stitching element.	**1.** **2.**	K-11
K-12	fabric fabric edges		Work weft-wise from right to left. 1. Come out at a and work a knotting stitch (K-2). 2. Go in at d and under the stitching element — come out at e and over the looped portion of the element. The knots are alternating direction with every other stitch. 3. The stitches and knots may be spaced or close, loose or tight. This would also work between two fabric edges.	**1.** **2.**	K-12

No.	Foundation	Names	Directions	Diagrams	Stitch
K-13	single warp floats stitch on fabric		Work warp-wise from top to bottom. 1. The needle slips from right to left under the warp and stitching element and comes out over the looped portion of the stitching element. 2. The needle slips from right to left under the stitching element and comes out over the looped portion of the stitching element. 3. The stitch may be close or spaced.	1. 2. 3.	K-13
K-14	pair of warps floats stitches on fabric		Work warp-wise from top to bottom with a knot on one warp and a wrap around the other. 1. Follow K-13 to work a knotting stitch on warp 2. 2. Slip the needle from right to left under warp 1 and then work another knotting stitch on warp 2 as in K-13.	1. 2.	K-14
K-15	row of stitches		Work rows of stitches upon rows of stitches to form a knotted fabric with diamond shaped meshes. The knotting stitches in the second row work upon the lags between the stitches in the first row. Follow K-13 for the knotting stitch.		K-15
K-16	warp floats stitches on fabric		Work weft-wise from right to left to form a knotted fabric with square meshes. (K-1)		K-16

No.	Foundation	Names	Directions	Diagrams	Stitch
K-17	warp floats stitches on fabric		Work weft-wise from right to left upon warp pairs. The pairs are exchanged with each row to form a knotted fabric with triangular meshes. (K-1)		K-17
K-18	warp and woven fabric		Work weft-wise upon warp pairs. The bottom weft is used as the stitching element. Work a knotting stitch upon each warp pair. (K-1)		K-18
K-19	fabric	French knot	Works to form a knot upon the element. 1. Come out of the fabric at a. Wrap the element around the needle. 2. The needle goes back into the fabric at b, inside the stitch. The knot is actually upon the element and does not bind to the fabric.	1. 2.	K-19
K-20	fabric	Chinese knot	Works to form a knot upon the element. 1. Come out of the fabric at a. Position the stitching element as in 1. Go in at b — come out at c under the looped portion of the stitching element. Snug up the stitching element before pulling the needle through. 2. A second knot is worked going in at d — out at e.	1. 2.	K-20

No.	Foundation	Names	Directions	Diagrams	Stitch
K-21	fabric	rosette chain stitch	Work weft-wise from right to left. 1. Come out at a. Go in at b and under the stitching element and come out at c and over the looped portion of the stitching element. 2. The needle slips up under the right leg of the first stitch, but not into the fabric. 3. Go in at d and under the stitching element and come out at e and over the looped portion of the stitching element.	1.　　2.　　3.	K-21
K-22	fabric edge		Work weft-wise from right to left along a fabric edge. 1. Come out at a. Go in at b — come out under the edge of the fabric, under the stitching element, and out over the looped portion of the element. 2. Slip up under the right leg of the first stitch. 3. Go in at c — come out under the edge of the fabric and the stitching element, and over the looped portion of the element.	1.　　2.　　3.	K-22
K-23	fabric edges		Work weft-wise from right to left upon two fabric edges. 1. Come out at a. Go in at b under the edge of the fabric and up under the edge of the bottom fabric and under the stitching element — come out at c, and over the looped portion of the stitching element. 2. The needle slips up under the right leg of the first stitch, but not into the fabric. 3. Go in at d — out at e and repeat the stitch.	1.　　2.　　3.	K-23
K-24	warp floats stitches on fabric		Work weft-wise from right to left upon warp. This is the same stitch as K-21, but upon warp. 1. Work a knotting stitch upon warp 2. (K-1) 2. Slip the needle up under the lag to the right of the first knot. 3. Work a knotting stitch upon warp 1. Slip the needle up under the lag between the two knotting stitches.	1.　　2.　　3.	K-24

No.	Foundation	Names	Directions	Diagrams	Stitch
K-25	warp floats stitches on fabric	multiple wrapped knot	Work weft-wise from right to left. 1. Begins like a simple knotting stitch (K-1), but the element wraps around the needle several times before being pulled through. Go under warp 4, wrap the needle, pull through. A second stitch would work on the next warp to the left.		**K-25**
K-26	fabric	multiple wrapped knot	Work weft-wise from right to left. 1. Begins like a simple knotting stitch (K-1), but the element wraps around the needle several times before being pulled through. Come out at a. Go in at b, wrap the needle, pull through coming out at c. 2. A second stitch goes in at d — out at e.		**K-26**
K-27	single element	multiple wrapped knot	Works a multiple wrapped knot upon the single element. 1. Position the element as in 1. Wrap the needle with the element several times, and then pull the needle through.		**K-27**
K-28	fabric edges	multiple wrapped knot	Work weft-wise from right to left between two fabric edges. 1. Come out at a on the upper fabric. Go in at b and under the edge of the fabric, come out at c. Wrap the needle with the element. Pull the needle through. Hold the wraps gently with your fingers and roll the needle back and forth as you gently pull through.		**K-28**

No.	Foundation	Names	Directions	Diagrams	Stitch
K-29	warp and woven fabric	multiple wrapped knot	Work weft-wise from right to left upon warp pairs. 1. Use the bottom weft as a stitching element. Work a multiple wrapped knot upon each warp pair.		**K-29**
K-30	fabric	bullion knot	Works a single multiple wrapped knot. 1. Come out at a. Go in at b — back out at a and wrap the needle several times with the stitching element. 2. Pull the needle through the wraps. Hold the wraps gently with your fingers and roll the needle back and forth as you pull through. 3. Go back into the fabric at b.	**1.** **2.** **3.**	**K-30**
K-31	fabric edges	bullion knot	Works a single multiple wrapped knot between two fabric edges. 1. Follow the instructions above (K-30). Come out at a. Go in at b, under the edges of both fabrics and back out at a. 2. Wrap the needle with the element. Pull the needle through. 3. Go back into the fabric at b — come out at c.	**1.** **2.** **3.**	**K-31**
K-32	fabric edges		Combines a multiple wrapping with a Van Dyke stitch (W-22). Work warp-wise from top to bottom. 1. Come out at a. Go in at b, under the edges of the fabrics and come out at c. Wrap the needle and then pull through. 2. Go in at d, under the fabric edges and out at e. 3. Slip the needle from right to left under the x of the first stitch, wrap the needle, and pull through.	**1.** **2.** **3.**	**K-32**

No.	Foundation	Names	Directions	Diagrams	Stitch
K-33	warp floats stitches on fabric		Work weft-wise from left to right. 1. Position the stitching element as in 1. The needle slips inside the top of the looped 'figure 8', and under the warp, and comes out inside the bottom of the looped 'figure 8'. 2. The stitch forms a knot with a loop upon each warp.	**1.** **2.**	**K-33**
K-34	fabric		Work weft-wise from left to right. 1. Come out at a. Position the stitching element in a 'figure 8'. Go in at b inside the top of the 8 — come out at c inside the bottom loop of the 8. Pull the needle through. 2. Repeat the stitch going in at d — out at e.	**1.** **2.**	**K-34**
K-35	two elements	weaver's knot	Attaches two elements together.	**1.** **2.** **3.**	**K-35**
K-36	single elemen	slip knot	Ties a knot that is stable when pulled from one end, but pulls out easily from the other end.	**1.** **2.** **3.**	**K-36**

No.	Foundation	Names	Directions	Diagrams	Stitch
K-37	radiating elements radiating stitches on fabric		Work counter-clockwise around a set of radiating elements or stitches to form a 'spider's web'. Work a knotting stitch upon each spoke of the web. (K-1)	1.	K-37

Figure 138: "The web of our life is of a mingled yarn . . ."
—William Shakespeare,
All's Well That Ends Well.

BIBLIOGRAPHY

Adovasio, J.M. *Basketry Technology.* Chicago: Aldine Publishing Company, 1978.

Albers, Anni. *On Weaving.* Connecticut: Wesleyan University Press, 1965.

Ashley, Clifford W. *Ashley Book of Knots.* New York: Doubleday and Co., 1944.

Auld, Rhoda. *Tatting.* New York: Van Nostrand Reinhold, 1974.

Bath, Virginia Churchill. *Lace.* Chicago: Henry Regnery Co., 1974.

Beutlich, Tadek. *Woven Tapestry.* London: B.T. Batsford, Ltd., 1967.

Bird, Junius. *Paracas Textiles and Nazca Needlework.* Washington: The Textile Museum, 1954.

Black, Mary. *New Key to Weaving.* New York: Macmillan Publishing Co. Inc., 1957.

Bolton, Ethel Stanwood, and Coe, Eva Johnston. *American Samplers.* New York: Dover Publications, Inc., 1973.

Brown, Nellie Clarke. *The Priscilla Battenberg and Point Lace Book.* Boston, Massachusetts: The Priscilla Publishing Company, 1912.

Burnham, Dorothy K. *Warp and Weft, A Textile Terminology.* Toronto, Canada: Royal Ontario Museum, 1980.

Burnham, Harold B. "Catal Huyuk—The Textiles and Twined Fabrics", *Journal of the British Institute of Archeology at Ankara,* Vol. XV, 1965.

Constantine, Mildred, and Larsen, Jack Lenor. *Beyond Craft: The Art Fabric.* New York: Van Nostrand Reinhold, 1972.

Constantine, Mildred, and Larsen, Jack Lenor. *The Art Fabric: Mainstream.* New York: Van Nostrand Reinhold, 1980.

Costumes of the Manchu Court. Eugene, Oregon: University of Oregon Museum of Art, 1973.

Cressman, Luther. *Archeological Researches in the Great Northern Basin.* Washington, D.C.: Carnegie Institution of Washington, Publication Number 538, 1942.

Day, Cyrus. *Art of Knotting and Splicing.* New York: Dodd, Mead, and Co., Inc., 1947.

D'Harcourt, Raoul. *Textiles of Ancient Peru and Their Techniques.* Seattle and London: University of Washington Press, 1962.

Dillmont, Theresa. *Encyclopedia of Needlework.* France: D.M.C. Library.

Drooker, Penelope. *Embroidering with the Loom.* New York: Van Nostrand Reinhold, 1979.

Drooker, Penelope. "Tapestry and Embroidery", *Interweave.* Vol. V, No. 3 (Summer 1980), pp. 37-40.

Emery, Irene. *The Primary Structures of Fabrics, An Illustrated Classification.* Washington, D.C.: The Textile Museum, 1966.

Enthoven, Jacqueline. *Stitchery for Children.* New York: Van Nostrand Reinhold, 1968.

Enthoven, Jacqueline. *The Stitches of Creative Embroidery.* New York: Reinhold Publishing Corp., 1964.

Gervers, Veronika. *Studies in Textile History.* Canada: Royal Ontario Museum, 1977.

Harvey, Virginia. *The Techniques of Basketry.* New York: Van Nostrand Reinhold, 1978.

Held, Shirley. *Weaving.* New York: Holt, Rinehart and Winston, Inc., 1972.

Hoskins, Nancy Arthur. "Moorman Weave Variations". *Shuttle Spindle and Dyepot,* Vol. XIII, No. 49 (Winter 1981), pp. 6-9.

Hoskins, Nancy Arthur. "A Paracas Needle Technique", *Interweave,* Vol. V, No. 4 (Fall 1980), pp. 34-37.

King, Bucky. "Weaving as Related to Embroidery". *Shuttle Spindle and Dyepot,* Vol. 1, No. 2 (March 1970), pp. 6-7.

Kybalova, Ludmilla. *Coptic Textiles.* London: Paul Hamlyn, Ltd., 1967.

Larsen, Jack Lenor. *Time Was and Is.* New York: Jack Lenor Larsen, Inc., 1979.

Mailey, Jean. *Chinese Silk Tapestry.* New York: China House Gallery.

Markrich, Lilo. *Principles of the Stitch.* Chicago: Henry Regnery Company, 1976.

Mason, Otis Tufton. *Aboriginal American Basketry.* New Mexico: Rio Grande Press, Inc., 1970. Original —Report of the United States National Museum, 1902.

Mellaart, James. "A Neolithic City in Turkey". *Scientific American.* April, 1964.

Michaels-Paque, Joan. *A Creative and Conceptual Analysis of Textiles.* Wisconsin: Joan Michaels-Paque, 1979.

Moorman, Theo. *Weaving As an Art Form.* New York: Van Nostrand Reinhold Co., 1975.

Nordfors, Jill. *Needlelace and Needleweaving.* New York: Van Nostrand Reinhold, 1974.

Opie, James. *Tribal Rugs of Southern Persia.* Portland, Oregon: James Opie Oriental Rugs, Inc., 1981.

"Practical Definitions for Three Openwork Techniques". *Textile Museum Journal,* Vol. IV, No. 4, Washington, D.C.: 1977.

Seagroatt, Margaret. *Coptic Weaves.* Liverpool: Liverpool Museum, 1965

Snook, Barbara. *Needlework Stitches.* New York: Crown Publishers, Inc., 1963.

Thomas, Mary. *Dictionary of Embroidery Stitches.* New York: Gramercy Publishing Company, 1935.

Tidball, Harriet. *Peru: Textiles Unlimited.* Freeland, Washington: HTH Publishers, 1969.

Tokugawa, Yoshinobu. *The Silk Road.* New York: Japan Society, 1977.

Wilson, Jean. *Weaving Is Creative.* New York: Van Nostrand Reinhold Co., 1972.

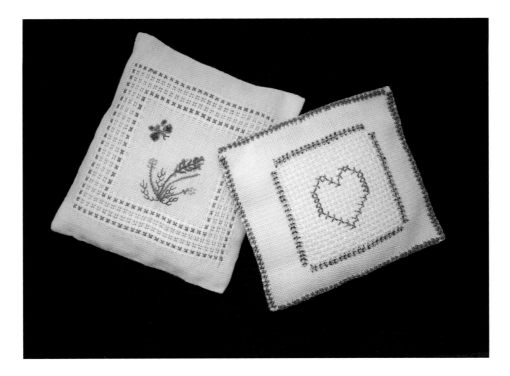

Lavender sachets of Bronson Lace and Canvas Weave are embroidered with floral and heart motifs. (W-2, W-46, K-19, K-26, L-46, L-4)

NOTES

1. Jack Lenor Larsen, *Time Was and Is,* (New York: Jack Lenor Larsen, Inc., 1979)

2. Irene Emery, *The Primary Structures of Fabrics, An Illustrated Classification,* (Washington, D.C.: The Textile Museum, 1966) p. 232.

3. Emery, p. 62, "an interlacing element simply passes under or over an element that crosses its path."

4. Emery, p. 214, "wrapping . . . a progressive encircling of one element or a set of elements by another element."

5. Emery, p. 31, "Looping is formed if the element crosses over itself as it moves on to form the next loop."

6. Emery, p. 39 & 43, "chaining . . . a simple progression of open loops drawn through other loops already formed by the same element."

7. Emery, p. 226, "a knot is a loop in an element through which the same element passes."

8. Emery, p. 27.

9. Emery, p. 27.

10. Dorothy Burnham, *Warp and Weft, A Textile Terminology,* (Ontario, Canada: The Royal Ontario Museum, 1980) p. 54.

11. Burnham, p. 87.

12. Burnham, p. 170.

13. Burnham, p. 179.

14. "Practical Definitions for Three Openwork Techniques", *Textile Museum Journal,* (Vol. IV, No. 4, Washington, D.C.: 1977).

15. Ethel Stanwood Bolton and Eva Johnston Coe, *American Samplers,* (New York: Dover Publications, Inc., 1973) p. 1.

16. Veronika Gervers, *Studies in Textile History,* (Canada: Royal Ontario Museum, 1977) p. 308.

17. Junius Bird, *Paracas Fabrics and Nazca Needlework,* (Washington, D.C.: The Textile Museum, 1954) p. 10.

18. Gevers, p. 311.

19. *Costumes of the Manchu Court,* (Eugene, Oregon: University of Oregon Museum of Art, 1973) p. 5.

20. Theresa Dillmont, *Encyclopedia of Needlework,* (France: D.M.C. Library) p. 502.

21. Raoul D'Harcourt, *Textiles of Ancient Peru and Their Techniques,* (Seattle and London: University of Washington Press, 1962) p. 50.

22. James Opie, *Tribal Rugs of Southern Persia,* (Portland, Oregon: James Opie Oriental Rugs, Inc., 1981) p. 148.

23. Harold Burnham, "Catul Huyuk—The Textiles and Twined Fabrics", *Journal of the British Institute of Archeology at Ankara* (Vol. XV, 1965) p. 169.

24. Luther Cressman, *Archeological Researches in the Great Northern Basin,* (Washington, D.C.: Carnegie Institution of Washington, Publications, Number 538, 1942) p. 58.

25. D'Harcourt, p. 57.

26. D'Harcourt, p. 60.

27. D'Harcourt, p. 124.

Boldface page numbers indicate location of definitions.